Accounting, Finance, Sustainability, Governance & Fraud: Theory and Application

Series Editor

Kıymet Tunca Calıyurt, Iktisadi ve Idari Bilimler Fakultes, Trakya University Balkan Yerleskesi, Edirne, Turkey

This Scopus indexed series acts as a forum for book publications on current research arising from debates about key topics that have emerged from global economic crises during the past several years. The importance of governance and the will to deal with corruption, fraud, and bad practice, are themes featured in volumes published in the series. These topics are not only of concern to businesses and their investors, but also to governments and supranational organizations, such as the United Nations and the European Union. Accounting, Finance, Sustainability, Governance & Fraud: Theory and Application takes on a distinctive perspective to explore crucial issues that currently have little or no coverage. Thus the series integrates both theoretical developments and practical experiences to feature themes that are topical, or are deemed to become topical within a short time. The series welcomes interdisciplinary research covering the topics of accounting, auditing, governance, and fraud.

Bernur Açıkgöz

Editor

Black Swan: Economic Crises, Volume I

 Springer

Editor
Bernur Açıkgöz
İktisadi ve İdari Bilimler Fakültesi
İzmir Katip Celebi Üniversitesi
İzmir, Turkey

ISSN 2509-7873   ISSN 2509-7881 (electronic)
Accounting, Finance, Sustainability, Governance & Fraud: Theory and Application
ISBN 978-981-19-5251-7   ISBN 978-981-19-5252-4 (eBook)
https://doi.org/10.1007/978-981-19-5252-4

This Springer imprint is published by the registered company Springer Nature Singapore Pte Ltd.
The registered company address is: 152 Beach Road, #21-01/04 Gateway East, Singapore 189721, Singapore

Preface

Crisis is defined as "*a difficult period, slump or depression seen in the life of a society or an organization in a country or between countries*" (TDK, 2019).

This book addresses all financial, fiscal and economic crises and their financial solution methods, which arouse from the complexity, instability and speculation of the economic and financial system since the 1600s, in the historical order in detail.

Before the discovery of Australia, it was impossible to imagine a black swan in the world because all swans seen before were white in colour, and so people thought all swans were white. When the first black swan was seen with the discovery of Australia, everyone was quite surprised. For this reason, the concept of "black swan" is used as a metaphor to explain the idea that some events that are thought to be impossible will produce more important and greater effects than events that are continuous or regular.

The "Black Swan" describes events that are thought to have a low probability of occurrence and are often ignored, or the events that create unexpected strong effects when combined with other possibilities, even if they are not ignored. The so-called "black swan" parameters can also be formed with the occurrence of random events. For example, the reason why many important events such as reform movements, industrial revolution, world wars and the economic crises of 1929 and 2008 are unpredictable can be attributed to the existence of black swans. The main reason why black swans are overlooked is that the people who lead the society have certain prejudices and trust in the correct functioning of the system.

The concept of the Black Swan, introduced by economist and risk analyst Nassim Nicholas Taleb in the book *Fooled by Randomness* in 2001, was used to describe the events that were thought to be impossible but had a huge impact when they happen. Some economists and investors have also used the term "black swan" to describe these crises due to the unpredictable and unavoidable nature and effects of economic, fiscal and financial crises.

This book aims to present to the reader all the economic, fiscal and financial crises in world history that have had a great impact and the fiscal measures taken by governments for each, in the historical chronology.

I would like to thank Melih Kabayel, who supported the book at every step, and Prof. Dr. Atilla İbrahim ACAR and Assistant Professor Metin Özdemir for their valuable contributions.

I would like to thank my esteemed teacher and my dear friend Prof. Dr. Ronald Harstad who guided and supported me at every stage of my academic life and read and gave his suggestions and contributions to this book.

I hope it will be of great benefit to all our readers…

İzmir, Turkey   Prof. Dr. Bernur Açıkgöz
2022

Contents

Editor and Contributors

About the Editor

Prof. Dr. Bernur Açıkgöz was born in 1979 in Ankara. After attending Ankara Finance High School, she continued her undergraduate studies at Dokuz Eylül University, Department of Finance. She received her master's degree in Financial Law from Dokuz Eylül University. In 2006, she was awarded her Ph.D. degree from Dokuz Eylul University Department of Public Finance. Her Ph.D. thesis covered the topics of poverty and development.

In 2006, she won the Harvard University Project scholarship and worked as a visiting professor at Harvard University. In 2009, she received a scholarship from the Swiss Government for a post-doctorate degree in economics at the University of Neuchatel/Switzerland and taught courses at Bern Universities. She then began to work in the fields of experimental economics and game theory, and for three consecutive years as a guest lecturer in the economics laboratory of the Montpellier University in Montpellier, France. Afterwards, she went to Missouri University, Indiana University and Arizona University with a scholarship from Missouri University. She then worked as a visiting professor at the University of East Anglia and took some courses from Exeter Universities in the UK with a Tubitak scholarship.

Prof. Dr. Bernur Açıkgöz has books, articles and papers on foreign direct investments, economic growth, panel econometrics, experimental economics and game theory. She is currently working at the Department of Public Finance and Financial Management at Izmir Katip Çelebi University/Turkey. In addition, Açıkgöz teaches at the Department of International Trade and Finance at Izmir University of Economics/Turkey and the Department of Economics at University of Life Sciences in Poznań (Uniwersytet Przyrodniczy w Poznaniu)/Poland.

Contributors

Açıkgöz Bernur Department of Public Finance, Faculty of Economics and Administrative Science, İzmir Katip Çelebi University, İzmir, Turkey

Boyner Merve Dilara Department of Public Finance and Financial Management, Graduate School of Social Sciences, Izmir Katip Celebi University, İzmir, Turkey

Çiloğlu Tuğberk Department of Economics/Post-Graduate Study, Graduate School of Social Sciences, Dokuz Eylül University, İzmir, Turkey

Kaya Muhammet Department of Public Finance and Financial Management, Graduate School of Social Sciences, Izmir Katip Celebi University, İzmir, Turkey

Kireçtepe Burhanettin Onur Department of Fiscal Law, Law School, Tokat Gaziosmanpaşa University, Tokat, Turkey

Kurtulmuşlar Mevza Department of Economics, Faculty of Political Sciences, Social Sciences University of Ankara, Ankara, Turkey

Kıral Halis Department of Economics, Faculty of Political Sciences, Social Sciences University of Ankara, Ankara, Turkey

Öztürk Alper Department of Public Finance and Financial Management, Izmir Katip Celebi University, İzmir, Turkey

List of Charts

List of Tables

Chapter 1
General Overview of Crisis Models and Financial Crises

Bernur Açıkgöz and Tuğberk Çiloğlu

Abstract This chapter will initially discuss the crisis models to better understand all the financial, fiscal and economic crises in world history. Considering the history of the world, each crisis, compared with the previous ones, has been based on different reasons and emerged in different economic environments. Therefore, new views and models have been put forward to explain new crises. However, these models are not interchangeable; they are rather complementary models.

Keywords Crisis · Financial crisis · Fiscal crisis · Economic crisis · First- second- and third-generation crisis

1.1 Introduction

The first part of the book will initially discuss the crisis models to better understand all the financial, fiscal, and economic crises in world history that are detailed in the following chapters, and then financial crises in general. The reason why the history of crises is addressed in this book from the 1600s is that crises before the seventeenth century are generally seen in the agricultural sector and are caused by production contractions, adverse weather conditions and transportation.

To understand crises better, first, it is necessary to become familiar with economic fluctuation and conjuncture. As is known, the economy follows a course with long-term fluctuations. This trend can be explained as a fluctuation composed of recovery, welfare, recession and crisis phases.

The conjuncture theory put forward, for the first time, by N. D. Kondratieff in his book "Long Waves in Economic Life", published in 1922, suggests that fluctuations

B. Açıkgöz (✉)
Department of Public Finance, Faculty of Economics and Administrative Sciences, İzmir Katip Çelebi University, İzmir, Turkey
e-mail: bernur.acikgoz@ikc.edu.tr

T. Çiloğlu
Department of Economics/Post-Graduate Study, Graduate School of Social Sciences, Dokuz Eylül University, İzmir, Turkey

are a process of 40–50 years. This theory was developed by Schumpeter and the economists who followed him. It argues that economic development in capitalism occurs in the form of big waves, one after another, and that the effects and results of each of these waves spread over a whole period and in time leave its place to the next wave of progress, and has been accepted for many years (Maillet 1983). Economic crises have generally been included in conjuncture theories and it is accepted that crises are the collapse phase of economic waves.

Considering the history of the world, each crisis, compared with the previous ones, has been based on different reasons and emerged in different economic environments. Therefore, new views and models have been put forward to explain new crises. However, these models are not interchangeable; they are rather complementary models (Çakmak 2007). We can group them under three main headings: (i) first-generation, (ii) second-generation and (iii) third-generation crisis models.

1.2   First-Generation Money Crisis Models

The first-generation crisis models, also known as the canonical (verified, standard) model, are the general name given to the first studies to explain economic and monetary crises. An article written by Paul Krugman in 1979 is regarded as the pioneering work of first-generation crisis models. However, his work is itself based on the work of Salant and Henderson. Salant and Henderson studied government policies and pricing in the gold market, working on commodity markets. Although they did not examine the money markets in their studies, their detections shed light on the functioning of money markets (Salant and Henderson 1978). After Krugman's work, this model was developed with Flood-Garber's work in 1984. For this reason, "First-Generation Models" are also called Krugman-Flood-Garber (KFG) models in international finance literature apart from the "Canonical Model" (Çakmak 2007). Flood-Garber's contribution to the Krugman model is that he analysed under what conditions and for how long a fixed exchange rate policy would last in a small and open economy (Flood and Jeane 2000).

First-generation models generally emphasized the importance of macroeconomic factors that initiated a crisis and considered monetary crises as the inevitable consequence of structural imbalances and inconsistent economic policies. For example, they accepted the unsustainable state policies formed by the combination of "expansionary monetary policies" and "fixed or semi-fixed exchange rate policies" that finance budget deficits by printing money as the most important cause of a crisis (Yay 2001).

In a more general way, models that suggest that financial crises are triggered by increases in budget deficits, in theory, are accepted as "First-Generation Models". These models suggest that if governments try to close budget deficits by printing money, the money supply in the market will increase, and as a result, if there is a fixed or semi-fixed exchange rate policy, this policy will lose its functioning, and thus will be followed by the foreign investors taking their capital out of the country and simultaneous dollarization in the country (Ickes 2004). As a result of increasing foreign exchange demand, central banks will have to issue foreign currency to the market, but after a while, this will lead to a decrease in foreign exchange reserves. This spiral will form the basis of a future crisis.

1.3 Second-Generation Money Crisis Models

The "Second-Generation Monetary Crisis Models", also known as "Self-fulfilling (Fuelling) Crisis Models", associated monetary crises with the reliability of macroeconomic policies. It is argued that sudden negative expectations regarding the sustainability of these policies create and fuel a crisis (Obstfeld 1984). This feature of self-fulfilling models is clearly demonstrated in Obstfeld's 1996 article: "The basic economic indicators are neither strong enough to prevent the speculative attack, nor weak enough to make the speculative attack inevitable" (Obstfeld 1996). According to the Second-Generation Money Crisis Models, it is a misconception that market actors (economic agents) assume that their own behaviour will not affect economic policy practices (Pasenti and Tille 2000). There is a serious interaction between the results of the current period and the expectations of the market actors, and this interaction is the focus of the second-generation models. The expectations of the actors in the market create an expectation across the market, and these expectations directly affect the macroeconomic policy decisions of the government, contrary to what is believed. If there is no optimism in the markets regarding macroeconomic indicators in the country, this will push the government to implement different macroeconomic policies, and even if there is no significant deterioration in the basic indicators of the economy, the expectation and the wrong policy applied in this regard may cause a crisis (Işık and Togay 2002).

The emergence of "First-Generation Crisis Models" is based on the failures experienced in the fixed and semi-fixed exchange rate regimes and stability policies implemented in Latin American countries in the 1970s and 1980s. However, the failure to explain the "European Exchange Rate Mechanism Crisis" (ERM) in 1992–1993 and the 1994–1995 "Mexico Crisis" led to the introduction of "Second-Generation Crisis Models" (Çakmak 2007).

For this reason, the second-generation, or "Self-fulfilling (Fuelling) Crisis Models", revealed that speculative movements and attacks on the currency of the country may cause crises even if the monetary and financial policies of the country are sustainable, i.e., even if there is no negative sign in basic macroeconomic indicators (Durmuş 2010). As we have stated before, the view that the expectations of the actors in the market will not affect the economic policies is inconsistent. Because the expectations formed in the markets directly affect the macroeconomic policies of the countries. The relationship between the expectations of the decision makers in the market and the result of the current period guides the functioning of the model. For example, if a fixed or semi-fixed exchange rate regime is implemented in the country and market actors expect a devaluation and this expectation pushes the state to raise the policy rates to protect the country's currency against devaluation, this policy will disrupt the government's cash balance. This deterioration in the cash balance will negatively affect the production and employment volume of the country. If the government must make a decision between maintaining the current parity and letting the parity drift, speculators in anticipation of devaluation will take positions in the short term and cause the devaluation to accelerate by disposing of the national currency. As a result, the government will have to give up the fixed exchange rate policy, and this sudden and compulsory change because of expectations could cause a crisis.

The main difference between first-generation models and second-generation models is the answer to the question of whether the timing of speculative attacks can be predicted. First-generation models suggest that sudden speculative attacks on national currencies are rational, indeed inevitable if the belief that the exchange rate cannot be sustained, hence the timing of speculative attacks is predictable. However, second-generation models emphasize that speculative attacks may or may not be rational, emphasizing that the timing of these speculative attacks cannot be predicted and points to the importance of expectations (Işık and Togay 2002).

1.4   Third-Generation Money Crisis Models

Third-Generation Models focused on the relationships between problems in the financial and banking sectors. With his studies published in 1998 and 1999, Krugman investigated the investment boom in the securities market and the effects of this explosion. In his study, Krugman (1997) emphasized that risky and excessive foreign borrowing and the unhealthy financial systems of debtor countries are the main causes of monetary, foreign exchange and banking crises. Various versions of Third-Generation Models have been developed in literature (Yay 2001): The first version of the model emphasizes that after financial liberalization, if the financial and banking system is not well regulated, problems such as moral risk (moral hazard) and excessive borrowing (over-lending), namely, hidden deposit insurance and hidden public guarantees can lead to the financial crisis (Mishkin 1999).

Banks' short-term borrowing in foreign currency, but long-term lending in national currency shows that there is both a currency and a maturity mismatch problem. In the event of such mismatches, the sharp and sudden depreciation of the national currency may lead to bankruptcies in the banking sector, then the bankruptcies will play a role in triggering a financial crisis by further reinforcing the negative expectations, uncertainty and insecurity in the financial market, or may lead to a deepening of an existing crisis. The 2001 crisis in Turkey is a good example of this statement of third-generation models. Because at that time, giving excessive loans to affiliates with interest rates below market interest was one of the weaknesses of the Turkish banking sector (Çakmak 2007). Also, exactly as the theory suggests, Turkish banks had high foreign exchange open positions, and the banking sector had both significant currency risk and suffered from currency and maturity mismatch as of November

2000. Almost all private banks (except Demirbank), which went bankrupt in the November 2000/February 2001 crisis and afterwards were transferred to the Savings Deposit Insurance Fund, went bankrupt for roughly these reasons.

Another version of the model states that crises are the product of bank panics. The fact that financial dynamics, which are known as self-fulfilling (fuelling) crises in Asian countries and are due to the pessimistic expectations of market actors despite sound macroeconomic indicators, caused bank panic and financial fragility, constituted another starting point of the Third-Generation Models (Çakmak 2007).

In Asian countries, which had very good economic indicators at the beginning of 1997, growth slowed in 1996 and some signs of excess capacity were observed. However, none of them faced the necessity of choosing between employment and exchange rate as was the case in the UK, and the IMF made high growth forecasts for these countries just before the Asian Crisis. Therefore, this great crisis experienced by Asian countries was a surprise for economists and financiers (Stiglitz 2002). It is very difficult to find traditional indications in studies and statistical data even after the crisis that Asian countries were at risk of crisis or that the years 1997–1998 were extraordinarily risky. The models developed to explain the Latin America (1994–95) and Southeast Asian (1997–98) crises resulting from the inadequacy of observing the deterioration in traditional indicators are called third-generation crisis models with general classification. These models are based on the main idea that banking crises and money crises create a vicious cycle that feeds upon itself, emphasizing the role of the banking and financial sector, based on the Asian crisis, and trying to explain the spreading mechanism of crises between countries.

In this model, the government provides direct or indirect guarantees to banks, some of which are branches of foreign banks, that do not have strict budget constraints and provide collateral to overvalued corporate bills (Durmuş 2010). Most of the domestic companies also obtain loan financing by borrowing from foreign funds. In other words, the government provides support directly or indirectly to balance the financial system and encourage banks abroad. However, the lack of regulation and unsustainable policies of the government in the financial system creates moral hazard problems in the financial system and this triggers a crisis not predictable from macroeconomic indicators.

After briefly mentioning the crisis theories, we must emphasize that the financial system is vital for the healthy functioning of an economy, if we need to touch on the financial system and the emergence of financial crises in general. The main role of financial markets in the economy is to bring together economic units that supply funds with those that demand funds. This way, the amount of idle funds in the economy is minimized and the economic system works faster and healthier.

As can be seen, the financial system serves a very critical function in terms of the smooth functioning of economic activity. In cases where the financial system cannot fulfil this function, serious economic crises may occur. Throughout history, serious financial crises have occurred repeatedly, and have caused great damage to the real economy. Understanding the causes, developments and consequences of these crises is very important to avoid such crises in the future.

In general, we see that as the financialization trend increases, the impact and power of financial crises also increase. Financialization and financial globalization have significantly shaped the world, especially after the Cold War. With the increasing financialization and financial globalization, many developing countries have had access to foreign savings. Increasing financial globalization has been the source of serious economic progress in the eyes of individuals, companies and states around the world. For example, increasing financialization and financial globalization have made it possible for companies of all sizes, institutions, or governments to borrow at lower costs. However, besides all these positive effects, negative effects have also revealed themselves.

The process of integration of national and international financial markets that started after the Second World War and gained momentum after the 1990s brought the financial crisis phenomenon with it. During this period, when many developed and developing countries liberalized their financial systems and made their capital account open to the outside, serious increases occurred in the international movement of capital on the one hand, and long-term financial crises with rapidly expanding power and influence emerged on the other hand (Delice 2003).

As a result of increased financialization globally, the financial markets of most countries have become integrated. This integration implied that a financial crisis that could arise in any of these countries could spread rapidly to all countries to which it is related. For example, when a financial crisis broke out in country X and the financial assets of country X depreciated, the crisis also affected country Y, which had invested in the assets of country X thanks to financial globalization. In short, financial globalization and financialization is a reality that has both beneficial and detrimental aspects.

We can divide financial crises into two, local and global, considering their impact. Undoubtedly, as stated above, as financial globalization and financialization increased, the number of crises that had a global impact also increased. There is an important point to be mentioned here: Financial globalization alone is not enough for a crisis to have major global effects. At the same time, a country that has been integrated into the global financial system must have increased financialization within itself. In other words, the speed and density of transactions of the economic agents in the country in question regarding the financial system should be high. For example, the impact of the 2008 Crisis on the UK and on Vietnam was not similar. The UK was more affected by the crisis because the economic units in the UK have much higher ties with its financial system than the economic units in Vietnam have with its financial system. So, the degree of financialization in the UK is much higher than in Vietnam.

The first crisis that we can describe as global is the 1929 Crisis. American stocks, which rose rapidly during the 1920s and exceeded their intrinsic values, entered a big decline in October 1929. As a result, with the effect of leveraged transactions, sales rapidly intensified and the panic atmosphere spread to the whole country. Leveraged transactions played a leading role in the 1929 Crisis, as in most crises. For example, an investor with only $100 could make a transaction of $1000. He was borrowing the $900 from the intermediary institution or bank where he made the transaction.

Heavily leveraged transactions make a great profit in rising market periods but yield great losses if the market collapses. This happened during the 1929 Crisis. In the period when the stock market was booming, investors who used leverage/debt to speculate on stocks made huge profits. This attracted more investors to the stock market. More investors came to the stock market, resulting in stock prices exceeding their real values, and huge "price bubbles" occurred. But when things turned around, that is, when the stock market fell, the process was reversed, and leveraged trading was the biggest driver of the big crash this time around. As a result, the crisis was not limited to the United States of America (USA), it had an impact all over the world. Many financial institutions went bankrupt. This was followed by the bankruptcy of many real-sector companies.

The 1929 Crisis caused prices, production, employment and trade to move downwards. Some nations tried to solve the problems by taking such measures as raising tariffs and establishing unemployment insurance funds, to gain the trust of the public. However, the extreme price decreases experienced in 1931 overwhelmed these measures (Heaton 2005: 592–593).

Civilization progresses with the challenge-response model, that is, with the difficulties and the reactions and responses to these difficulties. The global system followed the same process when it came to financial crises. The crisis of 1929 was the first major crisis to be felt worldwide. The Federal Reserve (Fed) initially implemented a prescriptive monetary policy. According to the normative monetary policy, as the production in the economy increased, the money supply should increase at the same rate, and as the production decreases, the money supply should be reduced at the same rate. Such a policy was envisaged for price stability. For this reason, when the economy shrank and production decreased with the crisis of 1929, the FED reduced the money supply. This situation exacerbated the bankruptcies and collapse. Many organizations, already in a cash shortage, went into a deeper crisis with this policy. This policy made the effects of the crisis longer and wearier than expected. The FED tried to overcome the crisis by increasing the money supply much later, and it succeeded with this method. This experience was very important to the world. When the FED faced the 2008 Crisis years later, this time it responded more accurately and did not make the same mistake.

After the 1929 Crisis, the crisis that affected the world the most was the 2008 crisis. To understand the dynamics of the 2008 Crisis, it is necessary to go back a little. As it is known, the 1990s were a period in which information technologies rapidly developed all over the world. During this period, many technology companies offered their shares to the public on Wall Street. It was literally a period of "rush for technology shares". At the end of this process, the price of technology shares exceeded the underlying values of the companies. When the market saw this reality in March 2000, there were very hard sales in technology stocks and this process caused serious panic in the US capital markets. After this process, September 11 attacks occurred in 2001. Both events drastically reduced confidence in the American economy. In response to all these, the FED started to reduce interest rates to give confidence to the economy and to create a boom in the economy. This, in turn, sowed the seeds of the 2008 Crisis.

With the interest rate cuts of the FED, liquidity in the American economy increased significantly. This time the field of speculation was the housing sector. The increasing liquidity rapidly turned towards housing. House prices and land prices rose sharply, and a serious price bubble began. Brokers and financial firms started to demand housing for speculation, not for use. For this purpose, the use of mortgage loans from banks increased rapidly. If the price bubble in question had remained at this stage, it would probably not have been such a major crisis. However, the events that would create the real crisis started after that.

Commercial banks borrowed and gave new loans by securitizing and collateralizing their mortgage loans to provide more mortgages. Securitization of mortgage loans is one of the biggest factors in the spread of the 2008 crisis around the world. Banks issued and borrowed bills/bonds based on mortgage loans. Other commercial banks, on the other hand, did not only lend mortgage loans, but also purchased these mortgage-backed securities themselves. Subsequently, they developed second- and third-degree derivative products by securitizing the mortgage-backed securities they purchased themselves. Banks, investment banks and financial institutions have invested in these securities by borrowing/using leverage. As real estate prices rose, people were repaying their loan debts and the value of these securities was gradually increasing. After a while, banks started to give "subprime" mortgage loans with high-interest yields to low-income people, as well as people with sufficient assets. Since these newer borrowers had a higher risk, higher interest was demanded. But the only thing that made this whole system work smoothly was the ever-rising real estate prices that had already exceeded their real values. Because even low-income people were selling the houses, they were buying with subprime mortgage loans at high prices and paying their debts. However, the rise in real estate prices could not last forever.

In 2004, the FED started to raise interest rates again due to increasing inflation concerns. As a result, getting a real estate loan became more costly. Therefore, the demand for housing started to lose its strength gradually and the market realized that the housing supply had already exceeded the demand for housing in 2007. Panic spread in waves. Real estate brokers quickly started selling their properties. Prices fell rapidly. Sales accelerated further due to the leverage mechanism. First, mortgage loan interests to banks could not be paid, then mortgage-backed securities rapidly depreciated. This was what really started the collapse. Many commercial and investment banks that invested in these securities quickly went bankrupt or were on the brink of bankruptcy. As a result, commercial banks were unable to fulfil their essential function of lending to the real sector. The crisis quickly spread to the real sector. The financial collapse spread to the whole world due to rapid financial integration, immediately after, the European Debt Crisis started due to the 2008 Crisis.

The European Debt Crisis had a very complex structure. In this sense, the development process consists of multiple components, and its causes arise from various factors. Borrowing costs decreased due to the falling interest rates after the Euro was introduced as a common currency. This situation facilitated and encouraged the financing of public and private expenditures through borrowing. On the other hand, the decrease in the value of toxic assets held by banks due to the financial crisis and related uncertainties caused banks to experience financing problems. Aid given to banks by states to eliminate these problems increased national debt (Ulusoy and Ela 2014: 86).

The FED repeatedly launched monetary expansion programmes on a massive scale to overcome the crisis. As a result of the monetary expansion programmes initiated, a serious liquidity abundance was experienced all over the world. In response to the crisis, the American Treasury nationalized many banks and took on their debts. This way, the crisis in the USA was resolved within a few years. But the worldwide damage caused by the crisis has been enormous.

The monetary expansion programmes implemented by the FED to ease the crisis also negatively affected the stability of the world economy. There were intense liquidity inflows in many developing countries. These liquidity inflows artificially raised the national currencies of these countries and caused serious bubbles in the capital markets and bond markets. The FED signalled in May 2013 that monetary expansion will diminish, and then monetary tightening will begin. It then acted as it had signalled it would. In December 2015, it increased interest rates for the first time since the crisis began, because now the US economy had improved, and the low interest environment could lead to high inflation. After this move by the FED, serious foreign exchange outflows were seen in many developing countries and serious and rapid depreciation was observed in the national currencies of these countries.

Another factor that may cause various crises in the financial system in the medium/long term is negative interest application. The adoption of negative interest rates, which was initiated in Europe in 2014 and applied in Japan in 2016, represents an important turning point in central banking (Ünal 2017). After the 2008 Crisis, central banks of developed countries made a nominally below zero, i.e. negative interest repayment, for their debts from banks. The main purpose of the negative interest rate policy implemented by the central banks of developed countries is to prevent the funds transferred to banks because of monetary expansion from being re-deposited to central banks for interest income. Because, after the global crisis, the funds transferred by central banks to major financial institutions and banks were not adequately transferred to the real sector. Firms that did not expect real-sector expansion had preferred to stay liquid and reinvested their funds in banks to earn interest income. The negative rate policy managed to stop this trend significantly but caused possible medium/long-term vulnerabilities in the global financial system. Negative interest rates cause price bubbles in capital markets.

1.5 Conclusion

Although the financial crises in world history have many common elements, the main reason why theoretical models are limited in explaining financial crises is that the process of each crisis is different. Since theoretical models focus on different dimensions of crises, they can help us understand what the indicators of a crisis are, although sometimes they are insufficient to fully describe the process. It would be more correct to consider these models, which are stated as three separate generations, not as replacements, but as models that complement each other's shortcomings. Consecutive crises in the 1980s and 1990s formed the starting point of these three generations of models: the "First-Generation Models" linking the cause of the crises to the deterioration in macroeconomic indicators, then the "Second-Generation Models" claiming that the interaction between the expectations of the actors in the market and the government policies is experienced due to self-fulfilling (confirming) expectations, and finally "Third-Generation Models", focusing on the interaction between money and banking crises, which are also called the twin crises, can shed light on the crises experienced by complementing each other so that we can predict the indicators of new crises that may be experienced.

Instability risk created by the consequences of financial crises and by measures attempting stability, taken afterwards for the world economy, is quite important. Financial integration and financialization undoubtedly have many benefits. However, all these examples show that the movement of large-scale funds from one continent to another at the push of a button as a result of a financial crisis yields very risky situations. Against this, there are some measures that economic policy makers of developing countries can take. First, developing countries should develop moves to finance their economic cycles with foreign direct investments instead of portfolio investments that may exhibit rapid and unstable movement. In addition, rapid entry and exit of portfolio investments in a country in a way that creates instability in the economy should be prevented by various financial regulations. Long-term portfolio investments should be encouraged by tax reductions.

References

Çakmak U (2007) Para Krizi Modellerine İlişkin Bir Değerlendirme. Ekonomik Yaklasim, Ekonomik Yaklasim Association 18(62):1–31

Delice G (2003) Finansal krizler: teorik ve tarihsel bir perspektif. Erciyes Üniversitesi İktisadi ve İdari Bilimler Fakültesi Dergisi (20)

Durmuş S (2010) Sosyal Bilimler Enstitüsü Dergisi 5–2010(31–46):36

Flood R, Jeanne O (2000) An interest rate defense of a fixed exchange rate? IMF, Research Dept. Draft, March, pp 1–16

Heaton H (2005) Avrupa İktisat Tarihi (Çev. M. Ali Kılıçbay ve Osman Aydoğmuş). Paragraf Yayınları, Ankara

Ickes WB (2004) Lecture note on crises. http://econ.lapsu.edul-bickes!o::rises1.pdf. s.l-32

Işık S, Togay S (2002) Para Krizi Modellerinin Eleştirisi ve Uluslararası Para Sisteminin Düzenlenmesine Yönelik Keynesyen Öneriler. İktisat, İşletme ve Finans, Yıl: 17, Sayı: 191, Şubat, ss: 31–53

Krugman P (1979) A model of balance of payments crises. J Money Credit Bank 11(3):311–325

Krugman P (1997) What happened to Asia, 17 Nisan 2004 tarihinde. http://www.mit.edu/people/krugman/. Accessed 15 March 2021

Maillet J (1983) İktisadi Olayların Evrimi. Remzi Yayınevi, İstanbul

Mishkin SF (1999) Global financial instability: framework, events, issues. J Econ Perspect 13(4):3–20

Obstfeld M (1984) The logic of currency crises. Cahirers Economiques et Monetaries 43:189–213

Obstfeld M (1996) Models of currency crises with self-fulfilling features. Eur Econ Rev (40):1037–1047

Pasenti P, Tille C (2000) The economics of currency crises and contagion: an introduction. Fed Reserve Bank N Y Econ Policy Rev 6, 3(September):3–16

Salant S, Henderson D (1978) Market anticipation of government gold policies and the price of gold. J Polit Econ 86(August):627–648

Stiglitz J (2002) Küreselleşme: Büyük Hayal Kırıklığı. Plan B Yayınları, İkinci Basım, İstanbul

Ulusoy A, Ela M (2014) Avrupa Borç Krizi ve Türkiye İçin Öneriler. Hak İş Uluslararası Emek ve Toplum Dergisi 3(7):84–119

Ünal AE (2017) Parasal Genişlemeye Alternatif Arayişlari, Negatif Faiz. Politik Ekonomik Kuram 1(2):66–78

Yay GG (2001) 1990'lı Yıllardaki Finansal Krizler ve Türkiye Krizi. Yeni Türkiye, Kasım-Aralık, Yıl: 7, 2(42):1234–1248

Professor Dr. Bernur Açıkgöz was born in 1979 in Ankara. After attending Ankara Finance High School, she continued her undergraduate studies at Dokuz Eylül University, Department of Finance. She received her master's degree in Financial Law from Dokuz Eylül University. In 2006, she was awarded her Ph.D. degree from Dokuz Eylul University Department of Public Finance. Her Ph.D. thesis covered the topics of poverty and development.

In 2006, she won the Harvard University Project scholarship and worked as a visiting professor at Harvard University. In 2009, she received a scholarship from the Swiss Government for a post-doctorate degree in economics at the University of Neuchatel/Switzerland, and taught courses at Bern Universities. She then began to work in the fields of experimental economics and game theory, and for three consecutive years as a guest lecturer in the economics laboratory of the Montpellier University in Montpellier, France. Afterwards, she went to Missouri University, Indiana University and Arizona University with a scholarship from Missouri University. She then worked as a visiting professor at the University of East Anglia and took some courses from Exeter Universities in the UK with a Tubitak scholarship.

Professor Dr. Bernur Açıkgöz has books, articles and papers on foreign direct investments, economic growth, panel econometrics, experimental economics, and game theory. She is currently working at the Department of Public Finance and Financial Management at Izmir Katip Çelebi University/Turkey. In addition, Açıkgöz teaches at the Department of International Trade and Finance at Izmir University of Economics/Turkey and the Department of Economics at University of Life Sciences in Poznań (Uniwersytet Przyrodniczy w Poznaniu)/Poland.

Tuğberk Çiloğlu is a Ph.D. student in Economics at Dokuz Eylül University, Institute of Social Sciences. He worked as a research assistant at Izmir Katip Çelebi University, Faculty of Economics and Administrative Sciences, Department of Economics between April 2017 and October 2019. Tuğberk Çiloğlu graduated from Dokuz Eylül University, Department of Economics with a high honor certificate in 2015. Tuğberk Çiloğlu, who graduated from Dokuz Eylül University Social Sciences Institute, Economics Master's program in 2019, has been continuing his doctoral studies at Dokuz Eylül University since 2019. He has various academic studies in the field of economics.

Chapter 2
Dutch Tulip Mania: Tulip Crisis

Alper Öztürk

Abstract Considering world history from the fifteenth century; geographical discoveries have positively affected the economic functioning of European States. However, in the sixteenth century, the European economy did not exist much, and even the agricultural sector, where the highest production was made, declined. Later, the European States, especially the Netherlands, implemented modern agricultural practices, and this development brought about a change in monetary processes as a reflection of the improvement in agriculture. By the seventeenth century, European States underwent a great change with the reform and renaissance movements and the spread of colonialism. The transformation of European States into central states at the end of the seventeenth century and mostly at the beginning of the eighteenth century and the large amount of gold and silver stocks brought from the colonial lands positively affected their economies and these states began to have a say in the world economy in proportion to their economic power. The abundance of these monetary resources brought along the European States to act in line with different economic processes. This chapter addresses the causes, occurrences and consequences of the first period crises, which can be called the first real economic crises between the seventeenth and nineteenth centuries.

Keywords Dutch Tulip Mania · Tulip crisis · European states · Tulip market

2.1 Introduction

Dutch Tulip Mania, also known as tulip speculation, tulip bubble, reveals the period when tulip bulb prices in the golden age of the Netherlands between 1634 and 1637 rose to extraordinary levels and then collapsed. Tulip Mania is the first speculative bubble example recorded in history. Especially the increase in the price of rare tulip bulbs resulted in bubbles (Kindleberger and Aliber 2005: 9).

A. Öztürk (✉)
Department of Public Finance and Financial Management, Graduate School of Social Sciences, İzmir Katip Çelebi University, İzmir, Turkey
e-mail: av.alperozturk@gmail.com

© The Author(s), under exclusive license to Springer Nature Singapore Pte Ltd. 2022   13
B. Açıkgöz (ed.), *Black Swan: Economic Crises, Volume I*, Accounting, Finance, Sustainability, Governance & Fraud: Theory and Application,
https://doi.org/10.1007/978-981-19-5252-4_2

Tulip, whose homeland is thought to be Northeast Asia, moved from Asia to Anatolia, from Anatolia to Europe in the historical process was spread in Western Europe in the mid-sixteenth century. With the spread of tulips in Europe, the admiration of Europeans for tulips increased, and over time, the tulip became an indicator of wealth for Europeans. Between 1634 and 37, there was an unusual fall following an unusual rise in tulip bulb prices in Europe. In February 1637, the peak period of the Tulip Mania, some tulip bulbs were sold for a worker's annual wage or for a luxury home price for that day. Tulip Mania was first known for the third part of Scottish journalist Charles Mackay's book "Extraordinary Popular Delusions and the Madness of Crowds". According to Mackay, in 1636, a land of 50 acres was proposed for one of the Semper Augustus bulbs that had only two roots all over the Netherlands (Mackay and Vega 2000: 147-148).

According to the thesis put forward by Mackay; the majority in the Netherlands was wrong. This majority is anyone who hopes to be rich, including speculators. Mackay argues that, with the sudden drop in tulip bulb prices, investors suffered tremendous losses and the Dutch economy had a serious shock (Mackay and Vega 2000: 151-155). Although this work of Mackay is still popular today, there are objections from modern economists to his claims in his work. Many economists argue that the Tulip Mania incident is not as unusual as described by Mackay, and the price increases and decreases experienced did not result in bubbles.

Limited data from the seventeenth century, when the Tulip Mania occurred, have survived to date. In addition, most of the information about this event that has survived to date is subjective and it is difficult to research the economic order that occurred before, during and after the Tulip Mania. Economists were able to provide reasonable explanations for the extraordinary rise and fall of tulip prices in the Netherlands in the seventeenth century (Balı and Büyükşalvarcı 2011: 27). However, whether the Tulip Mania is a bubble is a matter of debate among economists.

In addition to the historical aspect of the Tulip Mania, it is important to consider it within the framework of economics. Tulip Mania, where there was an extraordinary rise and a very rapid decrease in tulip prices in the seventeenth century Netherlands, is the first bubble example in world history in terms of economics. This section will address Tulip Mania in terms of its historical and economic aspects.

2.2   Tulip: The Central Concept of Tulip Mania

The central concept of Tulip Mania is broken tulip. For the broken tulip to be understood, it is important to define tulip with all its features and to reveal the broken tulip accordingly. Tulip is a perennial plant with a bulb. A tulip can be produced through seeds or buds that form on the tulip bulb. When producing tulips directly by seeds, it takes 7–12 years for the seeds obtained from tulips to become a blooming bulb; whereas tulip bulbs produced by bud can bloom in 1 or 2 years. The tulip bulbs are planted between September and November. The blooming time of the tulip is from February to May, and it is removed from the soil in June and stored in a cool dry place. After the tulip planting, the bulb disappears when the bulb transforms into a flower, but a clone bulb and a few buds (baby buds) are formed in place of the lost tulip bulb. In production with buds, which is the main production method of tulips, tulip bulb increases in regular tulip bulbs at a rate of 100–150%. Tulip bulbs bloom in April or May, and flowers can be seen for a week. Tulips can be removed from the soil from June to September, but they should be planted again in September (Garber 2000: 39).

2.2.1 History of Tulip and Its Journey to Europe

According to taxonomy experts, tulip appeared in Pamir mountains and developed and diversified in Pamir Mountain and Tien Shan Valley. The plant tulip initially had an unadorned and solid (especially red) appearance and was shorter than the tulips today. It was also able to adapt to the harsh winter and summer conditions in Central Asia (Dash 1999: 17). The tulip was moved from its homeland to the Middle East, Caucasus and Anatolia with the migration of Turks (Dash 1999: 19). Tulip is a flower that is commonly grown by Turks and Iranians (Dash 1999: 35). With its entry into the Anatolia, tulip took its place in the decorative arts from the twelfth century and became an important figure in the decorations of the Anatolian Seljuk Empire and Feudal Principalities period. The first poet who wrote poetry verses for tulips in the thirteenth century is Rumi. In the fourteenth and fifteenth centuries, which were the first terms of the Ottoman Empire, quiet and secret love appeared towards this flower in Anatolia. Fatih Sultan Mehmed, the sultan of the Ottoman Empire, who conquered Istanbul in 1453, is also an important poet and is named Lalezar in his divan. Dursun Bey, the historian of the fifteenth century, wrote in his work titled "History of Ebbülfeth" that the importance was attached to gardens and tulips in Istanbul after Fatih Sultan Mehmed's conquest (Ünver 2006: 265). In the sixteenth century, it is seen that the most dominant flower was tulip in the wall tiles made in Anatolia. Tulip was not only limited to wall tiles, but it was also used as an important pattern in book, fabric, and fresco decorations (Dash 1999: 26–27–28).

Mike Dash suggests that the governor of Portuguese India, Lopo Vaz de Sampayo, might be the first to introduce tulips to Western Europe in the second quarter of the sixteenth century. In the work of Dash, this information is since gardening expert Charles de la Chesnee Monstereul told in the La Floriste François (Florist François) published in 1654 that Vaz took tulips from Ceylon to her hometown Portugal (Dash 1999: 34). Tulip came to Europe from the Ottoman Empire in the sixteenth century. Osier Ghislain Busbecq is generally considered to be the one who introduced tulip to the West. Busbecq came to Istanbul in November 1554 as the representative of the Holy Roman–German Empire and lived in the Ottoman Empire for 8 years. After returning to his home country for good, Busbecq published his memories as a book written in letter style in 1581 (Dash 1999: 36). Osier Ghislain de Busbecq, envoy of the Holy Roman–German Empire, who came to the Ottoman Empire during the reign of the Suleiman the magnificent to ensure peace between Ottoman Empire and the Holy Roman–German Empire, wrote in his letter from Edirne on September 1, 1555, that he saw some flowers like, tulips, daffodils, hyacinths on the Ottoman lands and these flowers bloomed when the weather is good despite the season, and he gave the following information about the tulip: "Tulips have little or no odour. But the beauty and variety of colours fascinates you". Busbecq also wrote in his letters that he was surprised to see that the tulip bloomed in the winter. Busbecq expressed his admiration for the tulip in this letter and took the tulip back to his homeland (Ünver 2006: 265). Busbecq does not mention in his letters that he took the tulip directly to Europe. Busbecq did not take any plants with him on his return from Istanbul to Vienna in 1562; he only took pictures of these flowers. Although he says that he sent many plants to Europe a few years before this return, he does not give information about what he sent. Whether there are tulip seeds in these samples sent is a matter of uncertainty. However, despite this uncertainty, historians such as Hammer, Braudel and sources such as 'Enoyclopaeflia of Britannica' agree that the tulip was taken to Europe by Busbecq (İnalcık et al. 1984: 202–203). It is generally accepted that Busbecq calls the tulip petals tulipan because the tulip petals look like a turban—Turks called "dülbend" and the Dutch called "tulband" (Dash 1999: 37). The first tulips that were taken to Austria were developed in Ausburg in 1559 (Ünver 2006: 266) The first tulip planting in the Netherlands is thought to have started after the Dutch botanist Charles de l'Écluse was assigned in Leiden University and founded Hortus Academicus in 1593 (Dash 1999: 52). l'Écluse is not the first to grow tulip bulbs on Dutch soil. But l'Écluse is the only person in the sixteenth century in the Netherlands, perhaps all over Europe, who can identify, classify and understand tulips (Dash 1999: 54). As tulip was a flower that grows in soft climatic conditions, Charles de l'Écluse planted a tulip collection that can be grown in the Netherlands with harsher climatic conditions, and thus tulip cultivation became widespread in the Netherlands.

As a result of botanical studies on tulips, a variety of tulips of different colours and types were obtained. Single-colour plain flowers such as red, yellow or white were called *Couleren*, the tulip group with at least four colours was called *Marquetrinen*, multi-coloured tulips such as pink or red on a white background were called *Rosen*, and those with violet or mauve patterns on a white background were called *Violetten*, red-, brown- or purple-coloured ones on the yellow background were named *Bizarden* and purple-coloured tulips with thick white border were called *Lacken*. The most demanded thirteen kinds of tulip groups during the period of Tulip Mania were Rosen, Violetten and Bizarden (Dash 1999: 56–57). The remarkable tulip bulbs with high demand, which have more than one colour, are patterned tulip bulbs that have bright colours and stripes because of the infection of the tulip-breaking virus, a type of mosaic virus. It was not known in the seventeenth century that tulips had lines and flame patterns because of the mosaic virus. As a result of this virus, the reproductive power of tulip bulbs decreases, and therefore, the production of these bulbs is limited. The fact that the production of tulip bulbs is limited also disrupts the supply–demand balance in terms of the tulip bulb market (Veen 2012: 5).

With the spread of tulips in the Netherlands, tulip quickly became a luxury item and an indicator of wealth and became the favourite of Dutch statesmen and scholars.

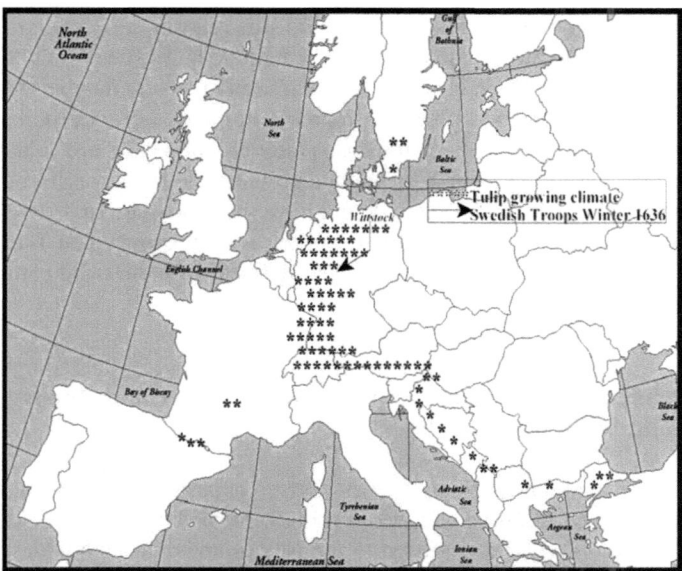

Fig. 2.1 Traditional tulip cultivation fields in Europe. *Source* Thompson (2007: 113)

The most admired and demanded tulip bulbs were the tulips infected by the tulip-breaking virus, a type of mosaic virus. These tulips were brightly coloured and patterned tulips, and they were given perfectionist names such as Dutch Admiral, General and Admiral's Admiral. However, these tulips were not as perfect as their names, and many species could not survive to date (Garber 2000: 41).

The map in Figure 2.1 shows traditional first-class tulip cultivation regions of the European continent in the second half of the sixteenth century. The map shows the beginning of the tulip's journey to Europe, starting from the tulip gardens in Istanbul and its settlement in the plains of Vienna and West Germany with a mild climate (Thompson 2007: 113–114).

2.2.1.1 Broken Tulip

Tulips, as a rule, are of a variety of colours, the petals of which are monochromatic. However, because of breaking the tulip bulb, the petals of the tulip may have flecked, flared patterns. Although the reason for breaking the tulip in the seventeenth century, when the Tulip Mania occurred is unknown, it was revealed that the mosaic virus caused the tulip to break in the early twentieth century. As mentioned before, the reproductive power of a tulip that is broken because of the mosaic virus decreases. For this reason, most of the famous tulips of Tulip Mania have not survived. If a broken tulip is reproduced by seed, newly produced tulips may not be formed as broken tulips but may have a single colour. For this reason, the broken tulips were produced only through the bud, as the clone formed the bulbs (Garber 2000: 40–41).

As for the tulip plant, the mosaic virus spreads only through the bud, not through seeds. The mosaic virus slows down the reproduction speed of tulip bulbs. For this reason, it takes years to grow the glamorous patterned tulips that are valuable in the tulip trade. The new tulips, which are obtained when the broken tulip bulb with a certain pattern is reproduced by seed, do not have the same pattern. However, some of these newly produced tulip bulbs can be broken at an unknown date. If a tulip with a specific pattern is reproduced by bud, new tulip bulbs with the same pattern can be produced (Garber 2000: 40).

2.2.1.2 Political and Economic Structure of the Netherlands During Tulip Mania

It is important to study the political history of the Netherlands in terms of the period when the tulip came to Europe and the tulip market was formed in the Netherlands. The period when tulip was recognized in the Netherlands, became widespread, the tulip market was formed, and Tulip Mania was experienced coincided with the Eighty Years' War. When this war between Spain and the Netherlands was going on, the Thirty Years' War between Catholics and Protestants that would affect all of Europe broke out in Europe in 1618 and ended in 1648. While the Thirty Years' War damaged the Central European population, it also damaged European economies. With the end of the Thirty Years' War in 1648, the Eighty Years' War also ended and the Netherlands achieved independence. Also, between 1634 and 1637, especially the bubonic plague caused great harm to the Dutch society (Garber 2000: 22). On the other hand, during the Tulip Mania period, the Netherlands had a developed economic order in manufacturing, trade, transportation and finance sectors as well as an urbanized society. In addition, the Netherlands was a trade centre that had advanced financing mechanisms during the Tulip Mania and accommodated traders from all over Europe (Garber 2000: 23). In this period, the part of Europe outside the Netherlands consisted of agricultural societies.

According to Garber, except for tulip speculators, the bubonic plague between 1634 and 1637 might have triggered the Dutch Tulip Mania. The bubonic plague from 1635 to 1637 caused great damage to the Dutch people. In the light of data revealed by Garber, the bubonic plague caused the death of 14,502 people in Leiden in 1635 (33% of Leiden according to 1622 population data) 17,193 people in Amsterdam in 1636 (one-seventh of the population), it caused the death of 14% of the city's population between August and November 1636. (In the period when the Tulip Mania peaked) in Haarlem, the centre city of Tulip Mania. The response to the death threat caused by the plague epidemic between 1635 and 1637 is thought to be the ambition to become rich in Tulip Mania (Garber 2000: 37–38).

In the first half of the seventeenth century, the Netherlands had a unique national feature in Europe. This feature was that there was no caste system in the society. Hence, every Dutch in the Netherlands was believed to have the right to switch between segments of society. However, a peasant citizen who was born as a peasant in France or within the borders of the Holy Roman–German Empire would die as a peasant. Likewise, social status was acquired from birth and this status would continue until death. In the Netherlands, however, a peasant could be the richest man in the country, and workers with small capital could trade using this capital and become a merchant if they were lucky. This national structure of the Netherlands caused the poor and the rich to dream of making big gains in the Golden Age. This emotion was influential for the artisans and craftsmen to trade tulip bulbs, as well as the rich (Dash 1999: 87).

2.2.1.3 Tulip Mania Period

The reason why the tulip flower attracts great interest and demand in the Netherlands is that the tulip is richer in colour compared to other flowers, besides, it is an unusually durable flower, and thus, it can be easily grown by novice gardeners besides garden experts (Dash 1999: 64). In the seventeenth century, tulips became an indicator of wealth and luxury. Because the Netherlands became the richest country in Europe in the 1590s, and in the period called the Dutch Golden Age, a tremendous amount of money flowed into the country. Thus, the wealth of merchants—especially wealthy merchants—increased, which resulted in luxury consumption for enormously rising merchants (Dash 1999: 64–65). In this context, the wealthy merchants and artisans began to construct showy country houses in the outer parts of the rich cities of the Netherlands to experience this richness. These showy country houses brought along the creation of large gardens. The fascination with tulips made the tulip the most important part of these large gardens (Dash 1999: 68–69).

Considering the change and development of the tulip trade over the years, the tulip bulbs that were the subject of the tulip market in the 1630s were not rare tulip species such as Semper Augustus, but the sellers of the tulip market were professional flower growers. With the increase in the number of people participating in the tulip trade, the demand for the most precious tulip species increased, tulip prices started to increase due to the increase in demand, and this price increase gained momentum since the end of 1634, and significant price increases were observed throughout 1635. Within a period as short as one week, tulip prices doubled in the winter of 1636. The prices formed by the Tulip Mania peaked between December 1636 and January 1637. During this two-month period, the number of people entering the market increased, which resulted in an increase in the demand for tulips (Dash 1999: 92). An example of this price increase is Semper Augustus, the most famous tulip type of the period. The flower, which was 5,500 guilders in 1633, reached 10,000 guilders in January 1637 (Dash 1999: 93).

Due to the increase in the demand for tulips, the continuous rise of certain tulip bulb prices revealed that this is an important investment area. Thus, in the early 1630s, some types of recipients that were not flower specialists emerged. These buyers were made up of people who knew either little or nothing about how to plant and grow the flower. These people called themselves "florists" and their sole purpose was to make a profit by trading tulip bulbs (Dash 1999: 87).

Before 1635, the first florists realized that the tulip bulb trade was a profitable business. Rumours began to spread that florists were getting richer through this trade; newcomers to the market decided to use their luck in the tulip market. The authors of the books and brochures of the period stated that, in a common language, most of those who got into the tulip market were people whose profession was weaving. These weavers could enter the tulip bulb trade with the capital they obtained by showing their assets as pledges or mortgages or by selling looms. This capital of weavers made them advantageous compared to other craftsmen. However, after a short time, people from other businesses such as attorney ship, printing and clergy also started to take place in the tulip bulb market (Dash 1999: 88).

The main desire of every craftsman of the period was to trade the tulip bulbs and become rich. To this end, the craftsmen were able to collect the modesty capital that could be adequate to get into the market. Although the people in the tulip bulb market had little capital in their hands, their desire to risk all the money they had was strong. Accordingly, two main characteristics of the Dutch come into play: the urge to save and gamble. Although these two impulses seem to contradict in terms of their characteristics, Tulip Mania was born because of the interaction of these two impulses. Considering the existing uncontrolled spending fear of the Dutch and the general increase in welfare between 1600 and 1630, it turned out that a significant number of Dutch families had a significant amount of savings. However, just like the saving drive of the Dutch, the gambling drive influenced every segment of society. As Willem Uselincx, a merchant of the period, said, no Dutch would keep the money he would use to earn more money in an old sock. In this context, the Dutch were able to use all their money for risky investments or bets in order to improve their economic conditions in the Netherlands, which had a high population density at that time. The trade of tulip bulbs was also a risk-free gamble for the Dutch. Because planting and growing tulip bulbs were easier than fitting a horse with a horseshoe or working on the loom eighty hours a week. In addition, the steady increase in demand for tulip bulbs brought along a consistent increase in tulip prices, and the Dutch followed this process with the excitement of making money (Dash 1999: 89–90).

The tulip trade, as a rule, was carried out in the summer, when the tulip bulbs were removed from the soil when they were physically portable (Dash 1999: 96; Oran 2011: 157). However, the fact that tulip buds were subject to the sale process was the first way to overcome this rule. It takes several years for the tulip buds to mature. This helped to eliminate the traditional sales schedule dependency on the tulip bulb trade. As a matter of fact, with the increase in participation in the tulip market, pressure increased for the tulip bulb trade to be a year-long activity (Dash 1999: 96).

As of the fall of 1635, the tulip trade underwent a permanent and radical change, and the tulips were subject to the purchase and sale process when they were buried in the soil, at times other than the June–September period when they were removed from the soil. The unit used in the sales process was not a tulip bulb, it was a kind of bond on which the properties of the tulip sold were written and the date on which the tulip bulb would be removed from the soil and delivered to the buyer. In order not to make a mistake about the bulbs subject to the tulips sales, a sign showing the type, weight and owner of the bulb was planted next to the buried bulbs. The fact that tulip bulbs were subject to sales, including when they were buried in the ground, saved the buyer from the effort to grow tulips. However, this trade had some disadvantages; buyers were buying tulips without seeing them bloom, there was no quality guarantee for the tulips purchased and they could not be sure about whether the tulips bought existed or whether they belonged to the seller. The Dutch called the wind handle (wind trade) the period when the tulip bulbs were sold while buried in the ground; this concept meant, for sailors, to manage the ships in windy weather; for the stockbrokers, the profit that will be obtained because of the trade; for florists, the state that tulips can be sold without any restrictions and limits (Dash 1999: 97). However, the Tulip Mania revealed that the bond-based tulip trade was gambling that the control was not in the hands of buyers and sellers.

The Tulip Mania was a gamble that the tulip buyer committed to pay a certain amount of money to the tulip seller at a future date, betting on the future price of the tulip bulb. This sales transaction is a forward sale (Dash 1999: 98). After the tulip is planted, a bulb develops for six to eight months before it blooms and produces many buds. Tulip Mania started seriously after September 1636, when tulip bulbs were buried under the ground and tulips were not suitable for examination. In this context, some of the tulip buyers were committed to paying for the tulips buried in the ground and which they could not see when they bought. In such tulip sales, they made down payments in kind. As for the tulip trade, the contents of the down payments in kind were composed of goods such as home, land, furniture, paintings, suits, and coats (Kindleberger and Aliber 2005: 115–116). The tulips, whose prices rose incredibly during the Tulip Mania process, were broken tulips.

During the Tulip Mania, rare tulip bulbs with unique patterns were traded at high prices, ordinary tulips with a single colour were traded at a very low price. In the Dutch tulip market, the prices of rare tulips rose during 1636. As of November 1636, the prices of ordinary tulip types, other than broken tulips, started to increase. Because the only thing every person who flocked to the tulip market in the fall of 1636 had in their mind was to make money. In the Netherlands, Tulip Mania reached its peak in the last week of January and the first week of February 1637. Since the real tulip bulbs did not change hands due to the contracts made in the tulip market, the Dutch people humiliated this trade by calling it wind handle (wind trade) (Goldgar 2007: 322). Finally, in February 1637, the tulip bulb market collapsed upon a sudden decrease in the price of tulip bulb contracts (Chart 2.1).

Tulip price index for the period 1634-1637 created by Earl A. Thompson is given in Chart 2.1. Since tulip bulbs are planted in the fall and removed from the soil in the spring, the prices in the figure are the tulip prices in the contracts for the tulips to be delivered in the future. Thompson did not have price data between February 9 and May 1, so the shape of the price drop observed in this period is unknown. The tulip market collapsed in February, although prices are not known. Without a significant change in tulip costs or utilities, the tulip prices rose by 20-fold from November 1636 to the beginning of February 1637, and the 99.999% drop in tulip prices from

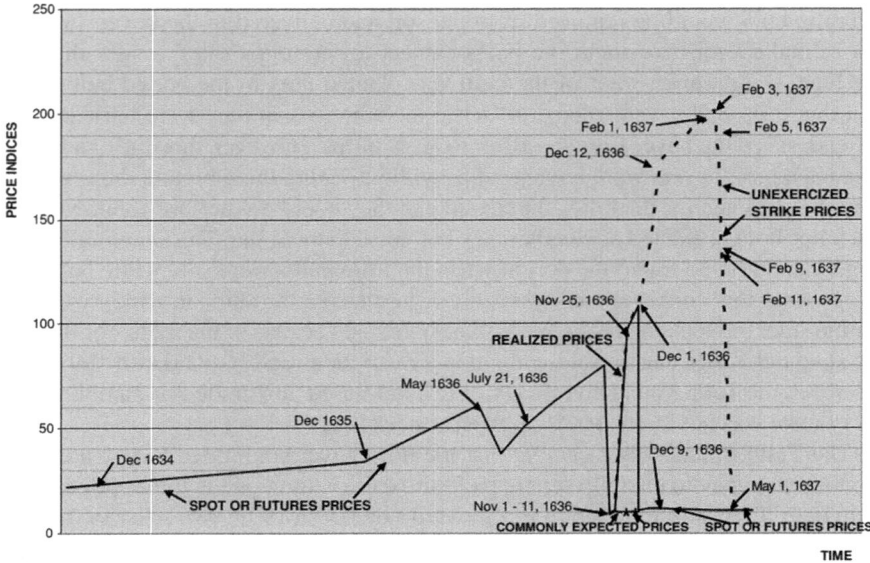

Chart 2.1 Tulip price index during the Tulip Mania (period 1634–1637). *Source* Thompson (2007: 103)

3 February 1637 to 1 May 1637, reveals that the 6-month period between November 1636 and May 1637 was a market bubble (Thompson 2007: 100).

2.2.1.4 Tulip Market

The Dutch economy collapsed in the 1620s when it continued its war with Spain after a twelve-year ceasefire, but it recovered impressively in the 1630s and the Dutch Golden Age began due to the enormous growth of the Dutch economy between 1622 and 1660 (Kindleberger and Aliber 2005: 116). There are many factors that ensure the successful development of the Dutch economy in the Golden Age of the Netherlands. One of these factors is the effort of to establish the economic order through safe economic activities. In line with this effort, the Dutch administration tried to strike a balance between safe and unsafe economic activities. Because sustainable economic prosperity can be achieved through safe businesses, whereas growth depends on risky economic enterprises. Stock trading transactions involving spot transactions, stock options and futures transactions are risky transactions. The Netherlands administration issued a decree banning insecure economic activities in 1610 because the stock trading transactions were open to manipulative transactions and speculative transactions were made in 1606 on the East India Company. The mentioned decree prohibited the sales transactions, that are, futures transactions—wind trade—on shares not owned by the seller. In other words, the Dutch government considered futures sales as an immoral gamble. Accordingly, laws emphasizing the forward sale ban were enacted in 1621, 1623, 1624, 1630 and 1636, peak year of the Tulip Mania, respectively. Because during this period, tulips were delivered in June–September when the tulip was removed from the soil. Except for this period, tulip sales contracts were forward sales contracts, and traders signed a contract in the presence of a notary that regulated their purchase of tulips at the end of the season. It was both advantageous and very risky for tulip bulb sales to be of a forward sale nature. Because if tulip buyers had bought tulip bulbs forecasting that tulip prices would rise and if prices rose on the date of delivery of tulip, the buyer would be able to make big profits or suffer great losses if the prices drop on the date of delivery. The Dutch government regarded the tulip speculation as a clearly unsafe speculation that transformed a legitimate business transaction suddenly into a gamble. Forward sales transactions in the tulip market were illegal, as a rule. However, the Dutch government made 6 attempts, through legal regulations that prohibit forward sales, to end this practice, yet it was not able to enforce these prohibitions. For this reason, the courts also refused to examine disputes arising from prohibited forward contracts. In other words, these forward sales were not recognized by the courts (Garber 2000: 34–35; Dash 1999: 99).

2.2.1.5   Structure and Operation of Tulip Market

During the period of Tulip Mania, tulip bulbs could be removed from the soil between June and September due to their nature and they could be subject to spot sales during this period. At times other than this period, traders signed a future contract for buying tulip bulbs at the end of the season. In order to verify a particular type of tulip and to be able to trade tulips according to this information, spot trading of tulip bulbs had to occur in June, usually after the blooming period (Gisler 2012: 85). The fact that tulips are subject to sales contracts outside of the period when the tulips are removed from the soil brought about the formation of the tulip market. The reason for the merchants to purchase tulip bulbs other than the period when the tulip bulbs were removed is that the merchants aim to increase their profit margins in tulip purchases and sales due to the increase in tulip prices since 1634.

Tulips need to be traded in the form of bulbs, as tulips bloom in as short as a few days. In addition to the gradual development of professionalism in the tulip bulb trade, when the tulip bulbs did not bloom, the bulbs did not give information about the colour of the flower. To address this problem, Dutch bulb trader Emmanuel Sweerts prepared a catalogue containing the drawings of blooming tulips and published this catalogue in Frankfurt in 1612 under the name Florilegium. The catalogue described tulips with their Latin names and provided basic information about the colour and shape of the flower (Dash 1999: 79–80). These tulip books were important sales tools that enabled flower growers to acquire new customers in terms of tulip bulb trade and could steer customers to purchase new flowers (Dash 1999: 81).

Until 1634, vendors of the tulip market were limited to professional tulip producers. However, since 1634, the seller composition diversified, besides professional tulip producers, there were speculators and individuals from all segments of the society. As a result of the rapid increase in tulip prices in 1635 and 1636, professional growers saw new opportunities that were created to make money in the market and started selling the bulbs in their stock to the florists who flocked to the tulip market (Dash 1999: 102). In the Tulip Mania, not only the rare tulip bulbs were the subject of the tulip trade, but also the ordinary garden tulip species such as Gouda, Switzer, or White Crown, which are traded among the people, and their prices increased and decreased (Kindleberger and Aliber 2005: 115).

There are some reasons that increase the demand in the tulip market. Tulips spread south after the Netherlands and were appreciated in France. In this context, Tulip Mania was experienced in Paris in the 1610s. The nobles of the period competed to present the most popular, most beautiful, and rare tulips to women in the French palace. In this period, aristocratic women of France created a fashion by wearing tulips in their clothes; the tulip fashion that emerged in the French palace spread to the surrounding areas over time. In this context, the rarest tulips were considered as valuable as a diamond necklace. Thus, the demand for rare tulip types increased (Dash 1999: 62; Garber 2000: 43).

With the increase in demand for tulip bulbs, professional tulip producers started to sell bulbs at higher prices. Due to the trend mentioned above in 1634, the increase in demand for tulip bulbs in France caused speculation. In 1636, the Dutch created an official forward sales market in which the contracts providing for tulip delivery in June–September, when tulip bulbs were removed from the soil, were bought and sold. Merchants came together in taverns called "colleges" and traded tulip bulbs. Buyers paid 2.5% of the price of tulip bulbs to the sellers, not to exceed 3 guilders under the name of wine money. In this sales transaction, buyers and sellers made contracts directly with each other. Deliveries in this market, which would otherwise be made in 1636, were never made due to the collapse of the tulip market in February 1637. In this process, tulip enthusiasts who buy regularly for rare tulip bulbs did not take part in the speculative market (Garber 2000: 44). In Tulip Mania, rare tulip bulbs were mostly the subject of high prices and registered sales transactions (Gisler 2012: 86).

The main element of Tulip Mania is that the broken tulips are rare (that is, their supply is limited). The rarity of the most beautiful tulip species led the Dutch to own these tulip species (Dash 1999: 75). Weight standard of tulip bulbs was determined according to "aas" which was 1/20 of the gram, that is, "granule" in Turkish units. Tulips ranged from 50 to 1000 granules, depending on the species. Among the florists, the weight of the tulip bulb on the day it was planted on the soil, as well as the weight when it was removed from the soil, were written on the bonds that changed hands. In addition, there were columns in the notebooks, kept by the florists who sold tulips, showing the weight of the tulip bulb in granules. In the tulip market, heavy tulips were more prominent and have more buds; accordingly, they formed the collection of future tulip bulbs. In addition to tulips sold by weight, rare tulip bulbs were considered as piece goods and were especially traded on the market. The sales system in the

tulip market was in a certain order, but it was complex. For example, a tulip buyer
could buy a tulip bulb on the condition that it would be at a certain weight when it is
removed from the soil (Dash 1999: 100–101–102; Garber 2000: 43).

2.2.1.6 Available Information on Tulip Price

During Tulip Mania between 1634 and 1637, tulips were sold as piece goods and by
weight. Rare tulip bulbs were traded as pieces, while tulip bulbs other than rare tulip
bulbs were also traded considering their weight (Garber 2000: 49).

Contract prices continued to rise until the information that tulips were postponed to
the traders on February 2–3. Then, the prices declined until the actual postponement
of tulip trade in the market centre in Alkmaar on 5 February 1637. The date of 5
February 1637 was confirmed as the day when the tulip trade was first suspended
(Thompson 2007: 100).

Garber claims that the prices available in the Tulip Mania are a mixture of apple
and orange prices. The change in tulip prices during the Tulip Mania is arranged in
graphics in the study of Peter M. Garber. Garber created these charts based on the
data collected from the auctions of the time, tulip sales contracts recorded in notaries
and G&W dialogues. This study involves the price index charts of Semper Augustus,
Admirael van der Eyck and Gouda Buds tulip bulbs which are included in Garber's
study (Garber 2000: 49) (Charts 2.2, 2.3 and 2.4).

2.2.1.7 End of Tulip Mania

In the first week of February 1636, although tulip sellers thought how much higher the
prices of tulip bulbs could rise, there was a great decrease in tulip prices in Haarlem.
On 3 February 1637, tulip bulbs were not in demand in the tulip market and florist
groups suspended their purchase and sale transactions, which brought along panic in
the tulip market. Everyone on the market tried to sell the tulip bulbs they had. Panic

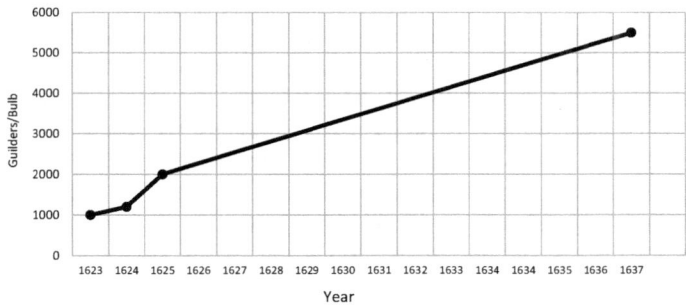

Chart 2.2 Price index of Semper Augustus in the Tulip Mania process. *Source* Garber (2000: 50)

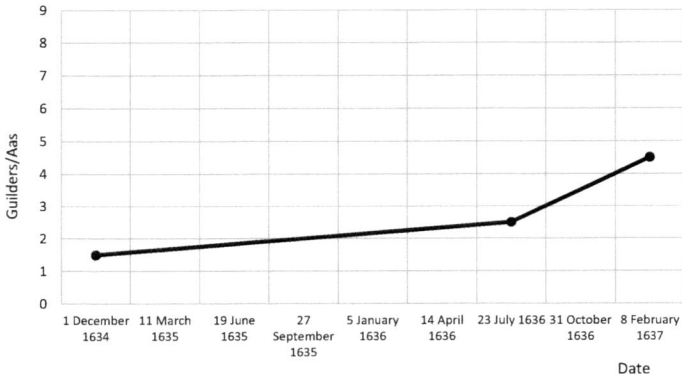

Chart 2.3 Price index of Admirael Van Der Eyck in the Tulip Mania process. *Source* Garber (2000: 50)

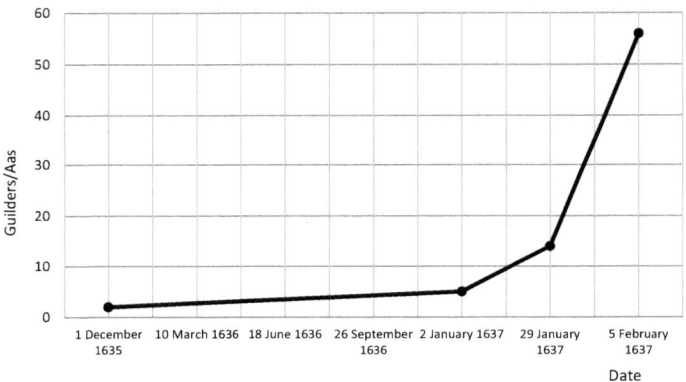

Chart 2.4 Price index of Gouda Buds in the Tulip Mania process. *Source* Garber (2000: 52)

spread to other states of the Netherlands within a day or two, and sellers could not find a buyer even though they reduced their bulb prices incredibly. The existence of the tulip market came to an end on the 5 of February 1637. The incredible rise of tulip prices from autumn of 1636 to February 1637, the increase in prices of even ordinary single-colour tulip bulbs on the market, and thus the absence of cheap bulbs in the market meant that the florists who would be new in the tulip market could not start work. The cessation of participation in the tulip market also brought about a collapse in the tulip market (Dash 1999: 134). On the day the tulip market collapsed in Haarlem, the market continued to develop in other states. However, with the spread of the news in other states other than Haarlem, tulip markets collapsed within a few days.

2.3 Measures Against Tulip Mania

Following the collapse of the tulip market, tulip growers and florists held a big meeting on 23 February 1637 to reduce their losses in the tulip market. Each of the cities and towns where the tulip trade was carried out elected its representatives in their local councils and sent them to this meeting (except Rotterdam, because Rotterdam sent a letter that it would comply with the decisions taken). In this big meeting held in Amsterdam, it was decided that the sales transactions made before the last bulb planting date were valid and that the buyers would have the right to terminate the contract by paying 10% of the first sale price in any sales transaction made since 30 November 1636. However, the problem was that this modest termination fee could not be paid by the buyers. Because tulip bulbs, which were bought from growers with a forward contract, were sold to other buyers with such contracts. The buyer's inability to collect his receivables because of the tulip trade resulted in that the growers could not collect their receivables. When it turned out that the problems experienced in the tulip trade could not be solved within the tulip market, high authority and state were needed to solve these problems (Dash 1999: 138–139).

The state administration took action to prevent a financial disaster that might result from the collapse of the tulip market. The local government in Haarlem approved three separate decisions in more than a month to resolve disputes between florists. In the first decree issued on 7 March 1637, all sales contracts made until the previous October within the city limits of Haarlem were cancelled; however, it did not introduce any regulation on compensating buyers' damages. Less than five weeks later, the first decree was withdrawn, and it was decided that the buyers were obliged to pay the sales price only for tulips purchased in food and beverage areas. One week after the second decree, the deputies in Haarlem changed their mind and referred the matter to the upper authority, the local parliament (the Dutch State Assembly in The Hague) and proposed the adoption of the compromise decision taken at the meeting held on 23 February 1637 (Dash 1999: 145).

The Netherlands State Assembly addressed the issue of compensating for the losses of tulip growers and florists as an issue that had no precedent and should have been handled carefully. Since the Netherlands State Assembly members had no knowledge of the case studies, the Netherlands State Council chose to take the matter to the Netherlands Supreme Court (Dash 1999: 146). The Netherlands Supreme Court completed its review of the Tulip Mania incident in the last week of April. As a result of the review conducted by the Supreme Court, they explained that they could not understand the reason behind the Tulip Mania and why the tulip market was out of control. The Supreme Court suggested that disputes between buyers, sellers, growers and florists be brought back to the local city administration and the issues be resolved as locally as possible. Within the scope of this proposal, it is recommended, for the resolution of disputes, that local judges first collect information about the tulip trade and start listening to the parties after having full knowledge of the tulip trade. In the meantime, judges were said to temporarily suspend all contracts related to the tulip trade until all information about the cases was obtained. If the disputes could not be resolved at the local level, they might apply to the Netherlands Supreme Court again. On 27 April 1637, the Netherlands State Council issued a binding decree that united all the main recommendations and was binding for all cities in the state. According to this decree, all tulip sales contracts made would be suspended until the necessary examinations and investigations on Tulip Mania were completed. The judges would be able to decide on the validity of the contracts concluded, after having sufficient knowledge. With this decision, tulip sellers would be able to find their lost customers and collect their receivables. However, state councils never collected sufficient information and problems remained unsolved (Dash 1999: 148–149). In May 1638, city officials set strict principles to resolve all disputes arising from Tulip Mania. In this context, buyers who want to get rid of their contractual obligations would be able to terminate their contracts by paying 3.5% of the first sale price. This was the most appropriate and feasible decision determined until May 1638. Disputes arising because of the Tulip Mania ended by means of this compromise. Almost all the disputes between florists and customers were resolved through compromise outside the court by giving mutual concessions (Dash 1999: 151–152).

2.3.1 Contemporary Opinions on Tulip Mania

After Charles Mackay, the Tulip Mania has been examined by today's historians and economists, and new views have been introduced on this historical-economic event.

According to Mike Dash, tulip mania was a madness, where ambitious and poor people lost themselves, and the Tulip Mania had no effect on the Dutch economy, contrary to popular belief. In this context, there was no general economic stagnation after this event and after the florists ended their debts, they did not have a big economic shock. After the Tulip Mania, most people have returned to how they were before the Tulip Mania. Because the profits of those in the tulip market through tulip contracts and the losses they faced on paper were comparable, even the richest florists did not face any legal penalty for not paying their debts. In addition, none of the tulip disputes before state prosecutors attracted attention and gained a great reputation, no judgments were made, and no one was convicted for these events (Dash 1999: 151–152).

Thompson argues that the century-old literature misrepresents the Tulip Mania, and in this context, this incident is not an example of "extraordinary popular delusions and the madness of crowds" put forward by Mackay. On the contrary, he claims that the tulip contract prices in the Tulip Mania are an example of the efficient market mechanism of what happened before, during and after the tulip mania (Thompson 2007: 109).

French argues that the Tulip Mania story is not only about the tulip bulbs and the price movements of these tulip bulbs and examining the basics of the tulip market will not explain the formation of the speculative bubble. According to French, tulip prices increased because of a government policy that increased the money supply and thus created an environment for speculation and bad investment (French 2006: 11).

In his work, Garber aimed to investigate the structure and environment of the market in the period of Tulip Mania. The lack of data prevented Garber from reaching a solid conclusion. However, Garber's study shows that at least the tulip speculation is not a clear madness for most of the 1634–37 period. According to Garber, tulip speculation within the scope of common tulip bulbs is a potential bubble only in the last month of speculation. Accordingly, the nature of the tulip market, contractual commitments, and environmental events are so ambiguous that they cannot substantially reveal the "bubble" formation (Garber 1989: 558).

2.4 Conclusion

Tulip mania is the first speculative bubble of history that occurred between 1634 and 1637 during the period called the Golden Age of the Netherlands. During the Tulip Mania, tulip prices increased unusual and decreased suddenly.

The rise in tulip prices caused speculators and only-profit-oriented individuals to enter the tulip market after a while. While tulips were sold only by professional growers in the tulip market until 1634, novice florists started to take place in the tulip market as of 1634. New participation in the market from 1634 to September 1636 increased the demand for tulips. The increase in demand for tulips caused a steady increase in tulip prices. However, during the period between November 1636 and February 1637, the Tulip Mania peaked, and on 5 February 1637, the tulip market, which caused the Tulip Mania, collapsed. Participation in the tulip market increased unusually during the period when the Tulip Mania reached its peak, and ordinary tulips that were not broken became the profit element of the tulip market. However, the unusual increase in the prices of ordinary, single-coloured tulips that were not broken, ended the demand for tulips as it resulted in the inability of new entrants to the tulip market to buy tulip bulbs. Price drops on 3 February 1637 caused panic. The resulting panic brought along a sudden incredible drop in prices because everyone was trying to sell tulip bulbs in the market and the demand for the tulip market ended. The tulip market collapsed on 5 February 1637 because of panic spilling over to other cities that started in the city of Haarlem.

As the tulip market collapsed, it was announced that all future contracts made after 30 November 1636 and before the opening of the cash market in the spring of 1637, would be interpreted as an option contract in accordance with the decision taken by the Dutch Florists' Guild. Thus, buyers could get rid of the contractual obligation and terminate the contract by paying 10% of the first sale price. However, since this decision did not end the disputes arising in the tulip market, Haarlem City Parliament, because of the one-year negotiation, regulated that the sales transaction contracts made between 30 November 1636 and spring of 1637 could be terminated by paying 3.5% of the first sale price.

There are many reasons for Tulip Mania occurring in the Netherlands. That the Netherlands was in its Golden Age in the first half of the seventeenth century, i.e., it was the trade centre of Europe, and the increase in the prosperity of the Dutch people brought along the increase in the tulip trade. In addition, the absence of a caste system in the Netherlands—which was common throughout Europe—brought with it every individual in the Dutch lands to enter the tulip market with the dreams of being rich, and to invest their modest wealth in the tulip market to be rich.

One of the most important reasons for the tulip market to be exposed to speculation, that is, the bitter end of the Tulip Mania is the sale of tulip bulbs contrary to their nature. In the traditional tulip market, tulip bulbs are traded only in the June–September period, when the bulbs are subject to spot sales, that is, when the tulip bulbs are removed from the soil. However, since 1636, the tulip trade was the subject of the forward market and in this direction, the purchase and sale of bulbs on paper by means of sales contracts such as bonds extended the tulip trade to one year. In addition, the sale of tulip bulbs without delivery, apart from the period when it was subject to spot sales, caused some problems in terms of the quality of tulip bulbs, whether the bulb existed or whether the seller was the owner of the tulip. In addition, it was a kind of bet as it was made for the purpose of making big profits in the future in the tulip market in future transactions. The person who made the forward sale could have made a huge profit on the delivery date of the tulip bulb or could have suffered a great loss.

It can be determined that Tulip Mania which occurred between 1634 and 1637 is a speculative bubble within the scope of the price information obtained. Especially in the period from 12 November 1636 to 5 February 1637, when the tulip market collapsed, tulip prices increased to form bubbles, and the collapse of the tulip market upon sudden fall of tulip prices on 5 February 1637 revealed that the bubble burst.

References

Balı S, Büyükşalvarcı A (2011) 1630'dan 2010'a Finansal Krizler Tarihi Balonlar, Panikler, Buhranlar ve Küresel Finansal Kriz. Çatı Kitapları, İstanbul

Dash M (1999) Lale Çılgınlığı. Sabah Kitapları, İstanbul

French D (2006) The Dutch monetary environment during tulipmania. Q J Aust Econ 9(1):3–14

Garber PM (1989) Tulipmania. J Polit Econ 97(3):535–560

Garber PM (2000) Famous first bubbles: the fundamentals of early manias. The MIT Press, Cambridge

Gisler M (2012) Tulip Mania? The Dutch tulip bulb episode (1636–1637) revisited. Schweizerische Gesellschaft Für Wirtschafts- Und Sozialgeschichte 27:79–96

Goldgar A (2007) Tulipmania: money, honor, and knowledge in the Dutch Golden Age. The University of Chicago Press, Chicago, and London

İnalcık H, Göyünç N, Lowry HW (1984) Osmanlı Araştırmaları IV. Enderun Kitabevi, İstanbul

Kindleberger CP, Aliber RZ (2005) Manias, panics, and crashes a history of financial crises, 5th edn. Wiley, New Jersey-Hoboken

Mackay C, De La Vega J (2000) Olağanüstü Kitlesel Yanılgılar ve Kalabalıkların Çılgınlığı-Karışıklığın Karmaşası. Wiley - Scala Yayıncılık, İstanbul

Oran A (2011) Balonları Daha İyi Tanımaya Çalışmak: Balon Tanımları, Modelleri ve Lale Çılgınlığı Örneği. Dokuz Eylül Üniversitesi İktisadi İdari Bilimler Fakültesi Dergisi 26(1):151–161. https://dergipark.org.tr/tr/pub/deuiibfd/issue/22731/242609
Thompson EA (2007) The tulipmania: fact or artifact? Public Choice 130:99–114. https://doi.org/10.1007/s11127-006-9074-4
Ünver AS (2006) Türkiye'de Lale Tarihi. Vakıflar Dergisi 9:265–276
van der Veen AM (2012) The Dutch Tulip Mania: the social foundations of a financial bubble. Department of Government College of William & Mary

Alper Öztürk is a Ph.D. candidate at Izmir Katip Celebi University and a lawyer who is a member of the Izmir Bar Association. He received his BA from the Department of Law, Dokuz Eylul University, Izmir, Turkey and Department of Economy, Anadolu University, Eskisehir, Turkey in 2014. He received M.D. in Public Finance with his thesis entitled as "The Evaluation of Conflicts Arising from General Enforcement Law and Tax Enforcement Law in Consideration of Jurisdictional Decisions" from Izmir Katip Celebi University, Izmir, Turkey in 2018. His research focuses on public finance law, taxation, public expenditures, economic and fiscal crises, and relationship of public finance law with other legal fields. Alper Öztürk has authored and contributed to book chapters and articles on these research areas.

Chapter 3
Bengal Bubble (1669–1772) and East India Syndrome (1669– –)

Mevza Kurtulmuşlar and Halis Kıral

Abstract The colonization process of fertile lands and countries in terms of production emerges as a fact witnessed in terms of both economy and political history. The Bengal Bubble in 1769 was also a result of the colonization process. However, when the Bengal Bubble crisis is examined, many firsts are observed in terms of economic history. Until this date, 1979, the country's governments were responsible for the devastating results of the colonization process. The most important factor in the colonization process that led to the Bengal crisis is the East India Company, which is a private company, unlike the others. Another distinguishing feature is that the first stock bubble in history was observed together with the Bengal bubble. It should not be overlooked that political figures also contributed to the said stock increase. Between 1757 and 1769, the overvaluation of the shares of the East India Company and a subsequent collapse gave its name to the financial crisis in question. The financial crisis in the company's stocks led to the collapse of the economy of the Bengal region, the inhibition of cotton and textile production and the subsequent Bengal Famine and, unfortunately, a syndrome that will not be erased from the memories of the society. This sudden decline in company shares, the structural economic crisis it caused, and its long-term effects take its place as the first case that strengthens the criticism about the limitation of the empowerment of international companies.

Keywords Bengal bubble · Bengal crises · Indian economy · British rule · Coins · Bengal famine

3.1 Introduction

Today's economy, where multinational companies direct world trade, has experienced numerous crises and collapses. The Bengal Crisis, which took place between 1769 and 1772, appears as a case lesson in terms of international companies and

M. Kurtulmuşlar (✉) · H. Kıral
Department of Economics, Faculty of Political Sciences, Social Sciences University of Ankara, Ankara, Turkey
e-mail: mevza.kurtulmuslar@asbu.edu.tr

© The Author(s), under exclusive license to Springer Nature Singapore Pte Ltd. 2022
B. Açıkgöz (ed.), *Black Swan: Economic Crises, Volume I*, Accounting, Finance, Sustainability, Governance & Fraud: Theory and Application,
https://doi.org/10.1007/978-981-19-5252-4_3

economic crises. As a matter of fact, this crisis is both a natural result of the business interests blended with the corruption of the British East India Company, one of the most important companies of the new age, and a dramatic example of how extreme Europe can go to reach the riches of the East.

The fact that the British East India Company, which came to the Asian continent to trade, guided the regional policy to protect its commercial interests and continued its existence for about 300 years still constitutes a historical example of the populist but justified reaction against multinational companies in India. Indeed, the Bengal Crisis caused by the company gave a striking blow to the textile industry, which was the apple of the region's eye, and the subsequent Bengal Famine caused the death of 10 million people in hunger and poverty and was not erased from the memories of the people of the region. Behind this cautious stance against foreign investors in the Indian economy today, there are companies established by Western countries to dominate the Asian market and the devastating economic storms that they bring.

Although the strong role of multinational companies in the global economy is engraved in minds as a universal motif with the British East India Company and the Bengal Crisis that it created, it has been observed that the same scenarios are repeatedly experienced in other places and times when we look at the economic history.

Reassessment of the Bengal Crisis and the British East India Company, which is the most important actor of the crisis, will also shed light on the current debates in these times when international trade, national and international economic actors and economic policies are re-discussed, and we even moved away from traditional policies in the global economic agenda of the twenty-first century.

3.2   Indian Economy

While the Indian economy is the world's most populous democracy with a population of 1.2 billion, it is also one of the fastest growing developing economies (Alamgir 2008). Considering that the country has reinforced its integration with the global economy with economic growth in the last 10 years, India will appear as an important power in the global sense in the near future.

It is estimated that India, which is the third largest economy in the world according to purchasing power parity, will rise from middle-high income country group to high-income country group by 2030 (World Bank 2020). The promotion of private sector investments and disciplined public finances help the country's economy to be positively differentiated from other developing countries.

Despite the favourable economic outlook, domestic and geopolitical risks create fragility in the Indian economy. India, which has a growing population, needs rapid growth in order to provide employment to this population. The fact that the said growth is sustainable and inclusive is vital for the elimination of income inequality observed in the country. With the pressure of economic and political changes on exchange rates and the threat of twin deficit on the agenda of today's Indian economy and policy makers, it is important that private sector investments continue without slowing down.

3.2.1 Indian Economy in Ancient Times

India is the settlement place of the Indus Valley Civilization in ancient times (3300–1300 BC). Trade and especially overseas trade have been on the agenda since the first stages of Indian economic history. While the fertile Indian lands played a major role in the development of agriculture and animal husbandry, simple metal tools and equipment were also traded. Evidence of urban planning, drainage facilities, and especially clean water supply also points out that the regional economy is supported by infrastructure work (Nehru 2004: 248). In this period, when precious metals are used as a medium of exchange, the Indian economy stands out as a developed rural economy.

3.2.2 Indian Economy in Mediaeval and New Age

The mediaeval age is emerging as a period of acceleration in international trade, and the ports of India are important logistical points in world trade that are worth fighting.

As observed in the whole Asian continent, the Indian economy is the source of important products such as silk, cotton, textile products, pepper, sugar, salt, spices and tea demanded by the world's households. The Middle Ages, which is the period when the richness, abundance and fertility of the East begin to dazzle the West, would bring developments that will have transformative effects on the Asian continent. The West, which demanded the glamorous products of the East with an endless appetite, did not have a product that could sell to the East in this trade. The need for importing products from Asia to Europe at a lower cost and reducing the trade deficits of European countries to manageable levels became the main determinant of the trade policies of Western countries. The control of trade routes and even the discovery of new trade routes were realized with these motives. The lands of India were on the agenda of the countries that were in the colonial race, both with their abundance and fruitfulness and because they were a busy stop in international trade.

Under the Mughal rule, the Indian economy had a detailed system of land income regulation, currency and trade policies. Gold, silver and copper coins were used in daily trade, but a free exchange rate was applied. The imperial mint was responsible for printing these coins. The stability of the central government enabled the empire to generate regular income with the simplicity of tax policy. The developed trade network within the borders showed that the regional economy was still a large economy, although it was dependent on the traditional agricultural economy. As a matter of fact, according to estimates, the per capita income of India under the Mughal rule in the sixteenth century is more than 1.24% of the per capita Indian income in the twentieth century (Moosvi 2015: 432–433). While 15% of the population of India lived in cities in the 1600s under the Mughal rule, this rate fell, under British rule, in the nineteenth century, contrary to expectations.

The collapse of the Mughal Empire and subsequent lack of political authority seriously damaged the country's economy. The Indian economy of the eighteenth century did not deviate from its goal of being a self-sufficient economy in the shadow of political instability and conflict. However, in this age of occupation and land acquisition, neither the Asian continent nor the Indian lands could prevent themselves from being the target of colonial empires. Regardless of the conditions of the period, international trade policies are a zero-sum game that each state aims to increase as much as possible for itself (Womersley et al. 2005).

3.2.3 Indian Economy Under British Rule

India came under British rule in a different way than other exploitation scenarios of the period. India's entry under the British rule was first with the commercial initiatives and then the arrival of British-based companies in the region. Although there are numerous European companies on the Asian continent, for Britain, in particular for India, this company is the British East India Company.

The most important reason why the British East India Company gradually dominated the economy of the region is the lack of political stability. The existence of fragmented political powers gave the company the chance to intervene in regional politics from taxation to agriculture and trade policies. British traders who focus on trade have a major role in reducing the share of agricultural production in the trade volume. The shift of capital and investments to the production of products that can be exported to the European continent led to both the decline of food production and the impoverishment of farmers. Considering the change in production policy and the death of the Indian people in hunger and poverty during the Bengal Famine, it once again reveals the importance of economic security.

British East India Company

The British East India Company has had a transformative role in global economic history. Bringing a new corporate identity to cross-border colonial activities, this pioneering company caused a global transformation with unorthodox military interventions and semi-dominant privileges. The company, which provides commercial benefits for itself in the region where it came to trade with its private army, has been a concrete example of the scepticism of international companies by destroying the trust in the political authorities of both the region and Britain with the excesses it applied. With its corruption, nepotism and corporate lobbying activities, the company, which succeeded in pouring the wealth of the East to London in nearly 300 years, is on the stage of history not only for India and Asia, but also as a case that every actor of international trade should learn from.

In the seventeenth century, the spice and silk trade were of great importance in world trade. Pepper, in particular, allowed the meat to be stored as edible and was in demand in the market as a necessity rather than a luxury consumption. Portugal and Spain were the pioneers of alternative searches in the spice trade thanks to their maritime power. Meanwhile, the Netherlands found itself under a commercial blockade as a result of the political turmoil it was experiencing and it was convinced that the only way to break this blockade was to reach the Asian continent and its riches by sea power. In 1599, Dutch ships returned from the Asian expedition with their storerooms full of pepper. The repercussions of this surprising development were reflected in the streets and markets of London, and the price of pepper almost tripled from 3 to 8 shillings (Milton 1999: 70).

The United Kingdom wanted a share in the trade of goods exported from the Asian continent. The profitable return of the Dutch from the Asian expedition, on the other hand, further motivated the British sea merchants and applied for a concession to Queen Elizabeth. Sea merchants, who wanted to be the biggest stakeholder in the pepper trade, finally obtained the concession they requested from the Crown in the last days of 1600 (Logan 2000: 308). The royal concession included these ambitious British sea merchants' bringing to Britain by purchasing, bartering, procuring and exchanging valuable goods from the West Indies.

From a political perspective, the Queen had given a concession that would allow "the development of commerce", and not just the commercial profits of a group of people, but a public benefit that would lead to an increase in Britain's share of international trade. The royal concession was granted for a period of time and had to be renewed every 20 years. The decision to establish a company, which would last about 300 years, was thus signed, although each renewal of the company's concession rights in the following years contained intense criticism and suspicions of corruption. As a result, the British East Indian Company was established with the permission and concession of the United Kingdom. This joint stock company, which was initially established for the purpose of conducting business operations with the joint capital and political permission of British sea merchants, gradually became a cross-border centre of power that monopolizes the economic activities of the Indian subcontinent.

The company, known as the "John Company" by the people since 1778, was not actually the first cross-border colonial company to operate in the Asian continent. VOC (Vereenigde Oost-Indische Compagnie), which was established by the Netherlands in the continent before the British East India Company, had many firsts in history. The company was a Dutch state-owned privileged corporation but was acting on the history stage as the world's first multinational corporation. This company, which had ventures increasing the appetite for profit for the Asian continent, would have an important place in the history of economy and finance as the first company to issue shares.

Apart from the Dutch, other states eager to deliver the fertile products of the Asian continent to Europe and America were also waiting at the door. This opportunity offered to the elite merchants of the country as a trade policy, especially by the Dutch and then by the United Kingdom, also stimulated the states that covet the economic benefits of other lands. Following the Netherlands and the United Kingdom, Sweden and Denmark also appeared in a way not well remembered in the economic history of Asia to establish their own Indian companies and operate in the continent.

281 investors collected 68 thousand 373 pounds of capital among themselves for four small ships that would set out in February 1601. The first stop of the expedition was not India but the islands of Indonesia, called the Spice Islands. The company, which established its first trade base in Bantam, made a profit of 155 percent with the expeditions between 1601 and 1612, and even the carnations sold only in the third voyage left 200 percent profit alone (Mukherjee 1974: 393). However, Britain's spice adventure in India did not continue with the same profit rates. The stagnation in the British economy, the escalation of overseas competition and the saturation of the spice market made spice exports no longer a profitable trade as before. On the other hand, the Dutch presence in Asia continued to grow stronger, and the British and the Dutch often came face to face. At a time when politics and trade were so intertwined, the Netherlands did not intend to give anybody the first place in the spice trade. Unable to stop the Dutch spice trade and its presence in the region with neither diplomacy nor military power, the Company had to acknowledge the Dutch superiority against the fierce competition. The company was taken out by the Dutch in 1682 from the base it established in Bantam. Thus, the Company, which left the spice trade and the East India Islands to the Dutch, found itself in search of a new market and region. While the withdrawal from the East India Islands benefited the Company both commercially and diplomatically, competition with the Netherlands fluctuated in the Asian field for years, reaching points that lead to a declaration of war between the two countries.

During the spice trade, the Company also received the concession of entering the Port of Surat from the Mughals through diplomacy. The company ventured to use military force against the Portuguese in alliance with the Iranians for control of the Gulf region. This military success would give the Company control of the Gulf Area and the route to India later.

Bengal, the centre of cotton textile production and trade in the seventeenth century, caught the attention of the Company. The demand for textile products, cotton and silk was still high in Europe. Deciding to continue its unfinished business adventure in the spice trade with the textile sector, the new route of the company was now Bengal-based India region.

For this reason, the Company did not hesitate to resort to military force, if necessary, to protect its commercial interests. What should be noted here is that the Company uses its own army of mercenaries to protect its own commercial interests over time, not the military power of the United Kingdom to which it is affiliated.

There were main reasons for the need for military power. One of them was that other Western companies operating in the Asian continent used similar methods. In state-owned companies, the need for military power was provided by the state army, and any attack against the company was made against the state. But this difference did not make a difference in the competition faced in Asia. The British East India Company was a royally privileged company but had no direct connection with the administration. So, although the British East India Company was a royally privileged joint stock company; in cases where diplomacy and commercial trumps did not work, it was inevitable to experience military conflicts due to the high-tension competition in the region. The company, which did not avoid using the gunpowder power to protect its commercial interests—which is one of the most important features that make the company colonial—had a different feature in the history of the economy with its military power.

For this reason, the company resorted to mercenaries in order to overcome the security difficulties it faced, and as its share of trade grew, the power of this private army formed by mercenaries increased. The strength of this private army owned by the company reached twice the army of the UK. The soldiers of the company, which had an army of 260 thousand people at its peak, consisted of both mercenary British soldiers and local mercenaries called Sepoy (Mason 1974: 125). The trade volume of the company was also incomparable with any British company. The British East India Company accounted for half of the UK's trade volume and thus had a much greater say in the formulation of trade policies than other commercial actors.

Of course, it is not a politically sustainable situation for a company to reach such a large trade operation, financial asset, and especially military power, even if it was established with royal privileges. Irish politician and philosopher Edmund Burke underlined that the company was an organization that threatened the existence of the existing order for both Britain and India, considering its extraordinary power of the company. Subject to repeated parliamentary inquiries, the Company protected the economic interests of its shareholders with an effort far beyond its time. An artificial optimistic picture was drawn with the corruption it has carried out, and the Company shares rose to high levels that could not be explained only by trade profitability. On the other hand, the Company taught corporate lobbying to the global business world. The consequences of the company's presence in Asia resulted in louder voicing of discomfort with companies that were inclined to manipulate politics in European countries of the time, and over time it was recognized as a threat to power and prestige. Even if the company's being taken over by the UK administration was the only way out, it was not so easy to take back the concessions granted when the company was founded. While the concessions were valid for 20 years, each time the concession was renewed, the Kingdom was charged with corruption allegations. As a matter of fact, the transfer of the company to the UK administration would not allow compensation for the damages it had caused, but it would be engraved in mind as a legacy that gave determination to the people on the way to India's independence.

3.3 Bengal Bubble, Crisis and Its Result

3.3.1 Formation of Bengal Bubble

For the East British Company, heading to Bengal had been a commercially lucrative decision. The demand for textile production, cotton and silk fabrics, where Bengal had a relatively superior advantage, was not likely to reach saturation as easily as in the spice market. As a matter of fact, Bengal's share in the trade of the Company was 12 percent between 1668 and 1670, while it reached 42 percent between 1689 and 1690, and reached 66 percent between 1738 and 1740. Thus, Bengal became the Company's largest supplier.

Many factors were effective in the formation of the Bengal bubble. The first of these was the Company's predominant role in the Asian market and its perception of being too big to fail. Especially in the UK territories, the power of the British East India Company was felt even on the British streets. The secret to the company's so much growth was, of course, the royal privilege and monopoly of trade with India, and the close and future-questionable relationships it maintained with the ruling class of the time. The company, founded with the concession, turned the political turmoil and instability in the Asian continent in its favour and turned the Indian lands based in Bengal into a British market for Asian products.

The Bengal bubble could not have grown without a Royal in need of public debt financing and an active and profitable stock market to provide that financing need. Considering the political instability of the period, the frequency of military conflicts and the need for security, trust in government bonds was quite low due to the political and geopolitical risks involved in lending to the state. In order to avoid these uncertainties and to finance public debt by capitalists, the UK provided tax concessions to lenders. Since this practice, which is reminiscent of the risk premium in the contemporary economic system, could not completely eliminate the uncertainties about the payment of the debt, lenders—in this case, the British East India Company—had to take beyond the age and innovative steps in order to keep the cycle of the stock market, corporate and public debt profitable.

At this point, the Company started to use the political power it gained by taking on the state debt to increase the stock prices. The management of the company bribed the politicians of the period with their stocks and, through this corruption, realized a speculative artificial increase in the stocks and was again sharing among its shareholders the profitability which was not based on any economic basis. This turned into a win–win game for both politicians and business owners. Thus, the British politicians were also forced to make an effort to increase the value of the company's shares and directed the expectations of small investors with optimistic rhetoric. Thus, public debts with the risk of non-payment were obtained with stock profitability with the help of politicians.

All these efforts paid off in a very short time. In less than 10 years, the value of the British East India Company's stocks had reached £200 million (Dale 2002: 40). Members of the parliament now not only maintained their optimism about the company shares, but they considered it as a personal interest to eliminate the political difficulties faced by the company. The fact that similar practices were observed in other countries of continental Europe attracted investors of all classes of the company shares in the UK. Every news from the Asian continent about the growth of the Company increases stock prices, and every investor, regardless of whether it is small or big, wanted to get a share of the wealth of the East. All these developments increased the company's stock demand excessively and stock prices were climbing.

Another factor in the creation of the Bengal stock bubble was the Bubble Act, passed by the British parliament. While the British East India Company was established, the number of companies in Britain did not exceed 20, but when this number increased to over 140 in 1695, the parliament passed the Bubble Act and an approval was required for the establishment of a company. This act, which prevents new actors from entering the market, was another reason for the upward movement in stocks, which has maximized the Company's chance to compete in Britain.

British East India Company shares, which were 39 pounds in 1698, were traded at 133 pounds in 1757. In 1768, shares hit 276 pounds, and investors were unaware that the value of Company shares peaked. A neglected asset bubble was ready to burst in the near future for the Asian continent and British investors.

Considering the fraudulent speculations and the financial and international trade markets that need to be regulated at the time, it is obvious that the bubble in question is inevitable. However, it is not possible to fully grasp the marginal effects of overvaluation and corruption in this price bubble, and even what the real market value of the company's stock value should be, given the lack of official records.

3.3.2 Bengal Bubble Crisis

It was not possible to predict that the Bengal bubble would turn into a crisis under the conditions of that period. Because the Company's survival, both at the point of renewal of concessions and in response to the corruption charges against them, strengthened the perception that it was a company that would not collapse. As a matter of fact, as long as the expectations and sentiments were positive, investors had no reason to cut their ties with the Company.

In the late 1760s, the Company was struggling with the political authority in power in India. The Mysore Kingdom, established in the south of India, obliged the Company to additional customs duties. This reduced the Company's profitability and share in Asian trade. On the other hand, the company, seeking a way out of corruption and bribery, did not want the problems experienced in the Asian continent to spread to the European continent.

On the other hand, although the Company, which owed its commercial profit to the relationships it has established, was pleased with the increase in the number of shareholders, that was not the case for major shareholders. The increase in the number of shareholders of the company caused the shares from the profits received by the major shareholders to decrease rapidly. This led to large shareholders starting to sell their stocks secretly.

When the news that the King of Mysore had seized the Company's assets in May 1769 reached London, the rumour that the major shareholders had put their shares up for sale was no longer a whisper. The fact that this news was heard by other investors suddenly drove optimistic expectations into panic selling. The intensity experienced in the purchase of shares this time turned its direction to the sale of shares. Artificial positive expectations gave way to pessimism on the verge of collapse. Investors trying to get out of this speculative scenario with the least possible loss had witnessed a rapid collapse in stock prices. Unfortunately, the bigger the bubble, the wearier the damage was. The company's shares lost 16 percent in the first month and 55 percent in the following months, reaching the bottom level.

The explosion of the Bengal bubble had devastating effects not only on the London Stock Exchange and the UK economy, but all over Europe due to the Company's international capital structure. Many people and companies across Europe have painfully awakened from the dream that the British East India Company was too big to fail. Yet no casualties would be as great and fatal as the loss in Bengal, the centre of the company and the crisis.

3.3.3 Bengal Famine

The times when Bengal was praised as "Heaven on Earth" by the whole East were over. With its abundance and fertility, Bengal, which the entire Asian continent had an eye on, would give its name to the famine that would turn into a famine disaster and would be a grave for 10 million Indians (Jonsson 2013: 167–170).

The extent of the damage caused by the British East India Company to Bengal was revealed by the drought in 1769 and the subsequent Bengal famine. Nobel prize-winning economist Amartya Sen described the Bengal famine in 1770 as a "man-made famine", drawing attention to the fact that there was no such famine before, drawing attention to the exploitative policies implemented by the British in the region through the East India Company (Sen 1997: 39).

Although the decreasing rainfall in 1768 did not pose a danger yet, reaching the level of drought in 1769 resulted in the crop failure of agricultural products. The fact that the authorities did not take the necessary precautions at the beginning of the drought was associated with the political environment corrupted by the Company, and the sacrifice of agricultural lands to the Company's industrialization policies was lately recognized mistake. The people of the region who gave up agriculture for more cotton textile production faced drought and famine and left their place to survive. Unfortunately, the textile industry came to a standstill with the famine in Bengal, which was the dream of Europeans with qualified textile products, and it took years to recover.

3.3.4 East India Company Syndrome

While the British East India Company, which started with the commercial adventure of British sea merchants, questioned the politicians, companies and even the colonization in Europe, the price paid by India was much heavier and irreversible. While the Bengal crisis and the following Bengal famine remained in the memory of the region, the widespread distrust and scepticisms towards foreign companies would enter the literature as the "East India Syndrome" indicating the British East India Company (Virmani 2004: 28). India, which learned in the example of Bengal that the wealth, power and uncontrolled industrial policies could have severe consequences without getting caught in the control mechanism, although the investments made by foreign and even multinational companies in the country have economic benefits such as increasing employment and contributing to economic growth, is still taking a cautious stance about multinational companies while determining its economic policies. Although this cautious stance in the international media is criticized as a populist discourse on domestic politics, it does not seem possible for India to forget the East India Syndrome, considering the suffering.

3.4 Conclusion

The colonization of India by the United Kingdom took place in a different way than the dominant methods of the period. India was colonized not by the political decision and military power of the United Kingdom, but by a British company established for profit. The presence of the British East India Company in India strengthened the Company's economic strength and even the UK was able to take over the management of the Company using military force.

The Titanic of the companies thought to be too large to sink, the British East India Company showed the entire financial world that the time when it was thought to be the most powerful was just before the sinking. It is not possible to say that financial actors have learned a lesson from this overvaluation-collapse duo when looking at the crises experienced later in the same cycle. However, this crisis was a lesson for the people of India, and the abolition of the company was an important symbol on the road to India's independence.

The Bengal Crisis is expected to serve as a reminder for those who want to learn from history in these times when international trade, economic security, states' trade policies and international companies are reassessed, discussed and even trade wars are mentioned.

References

Alamgir J (2008) India's open-economy policy: globalism, rivalry, continuity. Routledge, Oxfordshire

Dale SF (2002) Indian merchants and Eurasian trade, 1600–1750. Cambridge University Press, Cambridge

Jonsson FA (2013) Enlightenment's frontier: the Scottish highlands and the origins of environmentalism. Yale University Press, New Haven & London

Logan W (2000) Malabar manual. Asian Educational Services, New Delhi

Mason P (1974) A matter of honour. Holt, Rhinehart & Winston, London

Milton G (1999) Nathaniel's Nutmeg: how one man's courage changed the course of history. Hodder&Stoughton, London

Moosvi S (2015) The economy of Mughal Empire c. 1595: a statistical study. Oxford University Press, New Delhi

Mukherjee R (1974) The rise and fall of the East India Company. Monthly Review Press, New York

Nehru J (2004) The discovery of India. Penguin Books, New Delhi

Sen A (1997) Poverty and famines: an essay on entitlement and deprivation. Oxford University Press, Oxford

Virmani A (2004) Economic reforms: policy and institutions-some lessons from Indian reforms. ICRIER, New Delhi

Womersley D, Bullard P, Williams A (2005) Culture of Whiggism: new essays on English literature and culture in the long eighteenth century. University of Delaware Press, Delaware

World Bank (2020) The World Bank in India. https://www.worldbank.org/en/country/india/overview

Mevza Kurtulmuşlar is a research assistant and a Ph.D. Candidate at the Social Sciences University of Ankara in Turkey. She is working on Political Economy of Growth. Her current research investigates the relationship between economic growth and different forms of corruption such as nepotism, clientelism and lobbying. She received her bachelor's degree in economics from Bilkent University and her master's degree from Ankara Yıldırım Beyazıt University.

Halis Kıral is an Associate Professor at the Social Sciences University of Ankara (ASBU) in Turkey. He is also Head of Audit and Risk Management Department and Director of Center for Audit and Risk Management (ASBUDRM) at the ASBU. He was a visiting scholar in Duke Center for International Development (DCID) for the 2017–2018 academic year. He worked in the Ministry of Finance of Turkey as a state budget expert, public finance expert, head of the department of Central Harmonization for Internal Audit, and head of the Budget Policy Department. As the Head of Central Harmonization Unit for Internal Audit, his main responsibilities were to prepare and develop public internal audit and reporting standards, internal audit manuals, to arrange the certification and training programs of internal auditors and internal auditor candidates, to prepare quality assurance and development program and to evaluate the internal audit units within external quality assurance scope, to carry out designing, training, and monitoring processes of Public Internal Audit Software (İçDen©), and to identify and disseminate best practices of public internal audit units for 250 public institutions and almost a thousand public internal auditors and two thousand public internal auditor candidates. He has led several projects including developing Public Internal Audit Software (İçDen©) for public internal auditors and publishing Public Internal Audit Manual, Information Technology Audit Manual, Quality Assurance and Improvement Manual and Performance Audit Manual for Public Internal Auditors (the first manual in the world adopting the perspective of internal audit on performance audit). He has written several articles, books and book chapters on topics such as public finance, public financial management and control, specifically internal audit and risk management, and applied economics. Currently, he is also working on impact analysis, monitoring, and evaluation. He received his Ph.D. in economics from Hacettepe University.

Chapter 4
The Danish State Bankruptcy of 1813

Merve Dilara Boyner, Bernur Açıkgöz, and Burhanettin Onur Kireçtepe

Abstract In the background of major crises and bankruptcies, there is a series of events that dragged states into this situation. The devastating effects of the wars that lasted until 1813, and especially the Napoleonic War, lay behind the declaration of bankruptcy of the Danish State in 1813. In the 1700s and 1800s, when the wars were intense, the common problem of almost all the countries of the world was the financing of the increased defence expenditures during the war. Although Denmark was seen as a strong economy with commercial success in the said period, wrong decisions, monetary and political instability, high inflation made a great economic collapse inevitable. In the study, first, the effect of the Napoleonic Wars will be examined in terms of Denmark, and then the banking system that developed in Denmark and the reasons for the economic collapse will be included. Finally, the financial reforms announced after the crisis and the subsequent developments will be discussed.

Keywords 1813 Danish bankruptcy · Financial system of Denmark at 1810s · Affects of defence expenditures at Danish bankruptcy

4.1 Introduction

In the background of major crises and bankruptcies, there is a series of events that lead states to this situation. The wars that continued until 1813 and especially the devastating effects of the Napoleonic War lie behind the declaration of the Danish State's

M. D. Boyner
Department of Public Finance and Financial Management, Graduate School of Social Sciences, Izmir Katip Celebi University, İzmir, Turkey

B. Açıkgöz (✉)
Department of Public Finance, Faculty of Economics and Administrative Science, İzmir Katip Çelebi University, İzmir, Turkey
e-mail: bernur.acikgoz@ikc.edu.tr

B. O. Kireçtepe
Department of Fiscal Law, Law School, Tokat Gaziosmanpaşa University, Tokat, Turkey

© The Author(s), under exclusive license to Springer Nature Singapore Pte Ltd. 2022   45
B. Açıkgöz (ed.), *Black Swan: Economic Crises, Volume I*, Accounting, Finance, Sustainability, Governance & Fraud: Theory and Application,
https://doi.org/10.1007/978-981-19-5252-4_4

bankruptcy in 1813. In the 1700s and 1800s, when wars were intense, the common problem of almost all countries of the world was the financing of defence expenditures that increased during the war. Although Denmark was seen as a strong economy with commercial success in the period in question, wrong decisions, monetary and political instability, high inflation made the great economic collapse inevitable. The study will examine the effect of the Napoleonic Wars in terms of Denmark first, then address the developing banking system and the reasons for the economic collapse in Denmark. Finally, it will discuss the financial reforms announced after the crisis and the developments that followed.

4.2   Napoleonic Wars and General Political Situation Before the Crisis

The Napoleonic Wars are regarded as one of the greatest wars in world history. It is possible to say that the war covers the entire European continent in terms of its parties. In the process that started with the French Revolution, the rise of France was the trigger of this great war that continued from the end of the seventeenth century to 1815. Discussions about the exact date when the Napoleonic Wars started still continuing among historians today. However, Napoleon's coming to power with the military dictatorship in 1799 and the end of the peace process between the United Kingdom (UK) and France in 1803 (between 1792 and 1814) are considered as the beginning of the war (Colin 1994). The UK's war against France after the establishment of the Third Coalition consisting of Austria and Russia in 1803 is considered as the driving force that started the Napoleonic Wars. In the background of the UK's declaration of war against France, there was a discomfort that Napoleon changed the international system in Western Europe, especially in Switzerland, Germany, Italy and the Netherlands. The UK was particularly uncomfortable with Napoleon's claim to control over Switzerland. Similarly, Russia regarded Napoleon's intervention in Switzerland as different from other European countries and decided that the problem in question could not be overcome by peaceful methods (Kagan 2007). In this direction, the UK applied a sea siege to prevent the flow of resources from reaching France. Napoleon, on the other hand, responded to the UK with economic embargoes and tried to eliminate the coalition established against him.

The UK's first move against the Continental System that Napoleon tried to establish was to organize a naval attack against Denmark (Ryan 1953). An apparently neutral Denmark has been pressured to hand over its navy to the UK. The UK offered Denmark two options at this stage: ally with him or handing over his navy to the UK as proof of its neutrality. Napoleon's war tactic is; using the Danish fleet against the UK (Feldbaek 2001). During the French Revolution, the UK wanted to make sure that Denmark-Norway remained neutral and continued trade in and out of Danish waters (Yahil 1991). Therefore, in order to prevent Denmark from entering the war and being allied with France, he proposed that he would accept the occupation of Sweden and Norway would stay in Denmark. However, Denmark rejected all proposals and started the First Copenhagen War in 1801 (Thomas 2016). Although Denmark promised neutrality, the UK besieged Copenhagen in August 1807. After Denmark did not want to deliver its fleet to the UK, Copenhagen was under heavy bombardment for four days. The almost complete destruction of the city was enough to hand over the Danish fleet as British property and to destroy all ships under construction. Since Denmark did not have a navy, it attacked the UK with small boats and entered the war as an ally of France (Yahil 1991).

In addition, Denmark committed to stand by France in the war against Sweden. Russia invaded Finland and in 1808 tried to invade Sweden by declaring war against Denmark. The battle took place on the Swedish-Norwegian border after the British navy was prevented from passing through the Øresund Strait. As a result of the war, the Erfurt Congress was held in 1808 and an agreement was reached to divide the eastern part of Sweden into two parts by the Gulf of Bothnia and to include Finland in the Grand Duchy of Russia. Although France sent aid to Denmark in the war in question, it could not prevent this unintended result (Götz 2015).

The UK's move against Denmark's entry into the war as a French ally is the siege of the sea route connecting Denmark and Norway. Thus, grain shipments from Denmark to Norway were stopped and Norway's exports were interrupted accordingly. The cessation of Denmark's trade with the colonies and Norwegian exports had negative consequences both economically and politically. Isolation in Norway resulted in the economic crisis and increased poverty among the people. This was enough to persuade Norway's leading groups to leave Denmark and declare independence (Yahil 1991).

When the war ended in 1812 for Denmark, both the political and economic consequences of being an ally of the defeated France came to light. The cessation of trade and the severing of the bond with Norway, which had important resources, paved the way for the great collapse in 1813. As the losing party of the war, Denmark officially lost Norway with the agreement signed in 1814.

4.3   Development of Banking System in Norway

In the eighteenth century, the biggest problem of countries was budget deficits. Countries tried to tackle this problem in different ways. Increasing taxes, introducing new taxes or borrowing are among the methods used to overcome the problem. Both the eighteenth and seventeenth centuries were war times for Denmark-Norway. Therefore, public expenditures have increased considerably. First of all, in the period between 1755 and 1763, defence expenditures increased due to the Seven Years' War and the Napoleon Wars that continued until 1812. In addition, Denmark-Norway tried to adopt mercantilism during the period in question. Therefore, they wanted to both develop trade and pave the way for private enterprises.

In order to finance the development of trade, private banking initiatives were introduced by using the silver reserves obtained from the colonies. The first long-term example of this for Denmark-Norway was the Kurantbank. Even though there were attempts to establish a private bank independent of the state before Kurantbank, they were not successful. One of the reasons why banks have a special place in terms of Denmark-Norway is that it is possible for the state to borrow through banknotes printed as proportional to silver reserves.

In this respect, banknotes were printed by the state in 1713 to meet the increasing financing need due to the Great Northern War between 1700 and 1721. In addition, interest rates and capital demands increased in Denmark-Norway in the early 1730s. The first reason for this can be shown as the rebuilding of the city of Copenhagen due to the fire in 1728. Another reason can be the renewal of companies engaged in overseas commercial activities. Due to these developments in the markets and the desire of the Kingdom of Denmark-Norway to adopt mercantilism through more active economic policies in 1735, Kurantbank was established in 1736. The Copenhagen Transfer, Exchange, and Loans Bank were established as a joint stock company with the royal charter under the official name of Kurantbank. In 1737, Kurantbank started its activities in the Kingdom of Denmark-Norway, completely independent of the state, for the purposes of strengthening trade, production and contributing to the protection of the monetary system. During the period in question, Kurantbank and many of the banks established later gave loans over the bond discount and securities of deposit accounts. In addition, Kurantbank was given the right to print banknotes in 1736. Unlike other countries that gave banks the authority to issue banknotes at that time, the convertibility into the silver of banknotes printed in Denmark-Norway banking was possible. In addition, no restrictions were placed on the authority to print banknotes. Although the printed banknotes were not used as a mandatory payment instrument, they were used for payments to the government (Marcher et al. 2010). In addition, the nominal value of the banknotes printed by Kurantbank was kept very high and printed at least 10 rixdollars.[1] In addition to this, although there is no law in place related to making the banknotes proportional to reserves, it was possible to convert them into silver coins upon request (Abildgren 2006).

Although the government's share was very small at the beginning, Kurantbank created a loan volume of 500,000 rixdollars. The need for the state increased, as the attempts to convert banknotes into silver put pressure on the reserves of the bank. In 1741, the state started to increase the amount used through the bank in order for the bank to continue its activities. In 1742, 6–9% of bank loans consisted of the loan amount provided directly to the state. Due to the silver prices peaking in Europe in 1745 and the large amount of silver money leaking from the country, the government prohibited the export of silver coins abroad in the autumn of 1745. In addition, Kurantbank banknotes are called Courant banknotes, making them non-convertible payment instruments. The panic in the 1740s was overcome with the return of the silver price to normal levels and the narrowing of the credit volume. In the period

---

[1] Rixdollar is The Name Of The Silver Coin Used in The European Continent. It is Used As Rigsdaler Or Rijksdaalder in Danish. It will be Hereinafter Referred to as Rixdollar.

of 1756–57, although the bank continued to provide loans to the shareholders' debt rollover, the number of banknotes in circulation could not be brought under control and was not made proportional to the bank's silver reserves.

For these reasons, prior to the Seven Years' War, the bank was still in a weak position. The onset of the war caused the state to demand more loans, especially for financing defence expenditures. However, even though the bank tried to preserve its silver reserves, it was able to reduce the number of banknotes in circulation to only 4% (2 million rixdollars) of reserves. In 1756–57, the total loan volume of Kurantbank was 3 million rixdollars, 12–13% of which belonged to the state. But by 1762, the bank's credit volume reached 10.2 million rixdollars, 75% of which belongs to the state. Getting loans from national banks during the war times was a regular act at least Scandinavian countries (Winton 2012) and because of that no one gets alerted by the act of the state. As a result of the continuing increase in the credit demand of the state, Kurantbank was expropriated in 1773. With the expropriation process, it was possible for the state to manage its own debt, to save interest on loan repayments and to collect interest income from loans provided to private persons. However, the gap between silver and rixdollar widened due to the increase in the number of banknotes in circulation and the suspension of the convertibility of banknotes. In 1773, 1 courant rixdollar corresponded to approximately 20,634 g of silver (Marcher et al. 2010).

The amount of courant banknotes put into the market in 1737 was 233,000 rixdollars. This continued in six-digit numbers until 1744. But in 1744, the first largest expansion was observed, reaching 1,053,000 rixdollars. Although the number of banknotes in the market decreased relatively with the measures taken in 1745 and reached the level of 874,000 rixdollars, in 1747 it increased to the level of 1,101,000 rixdollars again (Chart 4.1).

Defence expenditures, which increased with the impact of the Seven Years' War, became apparent and especially after 1759, the number of banknotes in circulation increased rapidly. By the end of the war in 1762, the number of banknotes in circulation was at the level of 5,324,000 rixdollars. Especially after 1773, with the

Chart 4.1 Courant banknotes in circulation (1737–1787). *Reference* Marcher et al. (2010)

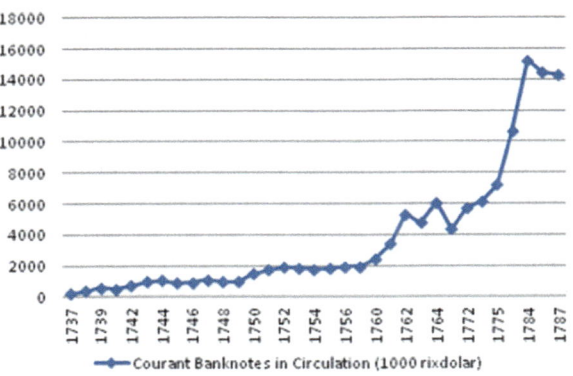

expropriation of Kurantbank, it is observed that the number of banknotes in circulation increased. While courant bills worth 6,143,000 rixdollars were on the market in 1773, this figure reached 14,318,000 rixdollars in 1787.

This expansion of Courant banknotes began to disturb the Duchies of Schleswig and Holstein and increased their desire to introduce more stable banknotes. Claiming VII. Christian's health, the king as of 1749, is not good, his son VI. Frederick unofficially assumed the king role (Bregnsbo 2014). The palace revolution in question paved the way for new monetary reforms. Thus, attempts were made to introduce more stable banknotes to the market.

Monetary reforms were first implemented by the Duchies of Schleswig–Holstein in 1788, and the state-owned Schleswig–Holstein Species Bank (The Schleswig–Holstein Species Bank) was established in Altona. Thus, Schleswig–Holstein Species Bank took over the functions of Kurantbank in the Duchies, and a separate currency was used in the monarchy. The said banknotes could be converted into silver. With the introduction of rigsdaler species, the rate of 125 courant banknotes to 100 rigsdaler species was determined and fixed. In addition, it is prohibited to use courant banknotes and to subject them to exchange at the mentioned rate (Abildgren 2006). The biggest reason for adopting such strict rules is that the Duchies were uncomfortable with the expansion of courant bills. The printing of money to finance the increasing palace expenditures and the expenditures caused inflation to rise. It is possible to say that the duchies want to protect themselves in this way from impending bankruptcy.

Another important development is the establishment of the completely private Danish-Norwegian Specie Bank in Copenhagen in 1791. This bank aimed to spread the species introduced by the Schleswig–Holstein Species Bank, which was established before, and to recreate the monetary union in a monarchy. For this reason, it adopted a stricter attitude regarding the number of banknotes it put on the market. In addition, they were free to use the courant value for the banknotes they put on the market or the market value of the species published by the previously established species bank. Although there is no obligation to use the newly issued banknotes in terms of special transactions in the market, they could be used for tax payments to the central government (Abildgren 2006). In this respect, it operated as a joint stock company, with similar strict rules to Altona Species bank. As a result of being a joint stock company, it could not have sufficient silver reserves.

With the international credit crisis in 1799, credits were severely restricted when the individuals wanted to convert their banknotes issued by the Denmark-Norway Bank of Species into silver. The bank, which could not survive any longer without state support, was closed in 1813. The monarchy continued to use the courant banknotes, which were released through the Deposit Institute (Marcher et al. 2010), to meet the increased expenditures. The fact that the monarchy did not help the Denmark-Norway Bank of Species was an important turning point in the panic of 1799. With the end of the Napoleonic Wars, the monarchy wanted to implement a contractionary monetary policy. Also, helping the bank while the war continued increased the cost of spending. However, despite all this, it was also seen that the monarchy could leave private banks alone (Chart 4.2).

Chart 4.2 Courant, Copenhagen, and Altona species circulation value. *Source* Marcher et al. (2010)

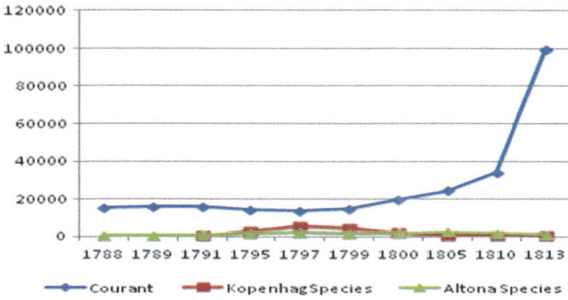

Although the circulation value of Courant banknotes in the market gradually expanded, the banknotes introduced by the Denmark-Norway Bank of Species, called the Copenhagen species, had a more stable value. In this respect, it reached a position with almost the same market value as the banknotes released by the Schleswig–Holstein Species Bank, which are called Altona species. In 1788, the value of courant was 15,072,000 rixdollars, while the value of Altona species was at the level of 197,000 rixdollars. In 1791, the first year of its establishment, the circulation value of the Copenhagen species in the market was 63,000 rixdollars, whereas the value of the Altona species reached 605,000 rixdollars and the value of courant 15,557,000 rixdollars. By 1813, the value of courant banknotes reached 99,090,000 rixdollars, while the value of Altona species reached 842,000 and the value of Copenhagen species reached 35,000 rixdollars.

4.4   Bankruptcy of Danish State and Financial Reform of 1813

The wars continued throughout the eighteenth century and finally the burden of the Napoleonic War put the state in trouble. Increasing expenditures, especially defence expenditures based on armament, pushed the state to seek financing. For this reason, borrowing was used as the first option. The rising trend in the chart below is the most concrete indicator of this. While the total debt was 1.5 million rixdollars in 1700, the debt amount increased to 47.1 million rixdollars in 1799 (Marcher et al. 2010: 131). Increasing defence expenditures was shown as the main reason for this increase (Chart 4.3).

In addition, Denmark became the trade centre of goods obtained from its colonies in America, Africa and Asia during the period in question. Especially during the Napoleonic War, the city, which was under heavy bombardment, had a hard time to carry out trade. Furthermore, although Denmark, an ally of Napoleon, received support from France, it mobilized country resources for the army and navy. Trade became unsustainable, causing the bankruptcy of shipowners and merchants living in Copenhagen (Wullschlager 2000). The rebuilding of Copenhagen and the navy

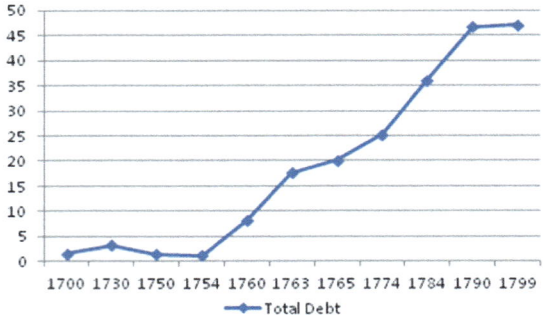

Chart 4.3 Total national debt graph (1700–1799). *Source* Marcher et al. (2010)

was financed by printing unlimited money, which caused Kurantbank to fall into a weak position especially between 1800 and 1812 and resulted in the white flag of Kurantbank in 1812 (Andersen 2011) (Chart 4.4).

As can be seen in the chart above, inflation was particularly high in 1813, when the collapse occurred. Examining the figures, while the inflation was 12.5% in 1808, it climbed to 55% in 1809. The increasing trend continued in 1810, with an inflation of 60.2%. Although there was a slight decrease in 1811, the increase was more than the previous years, being 86.8% in 1812. However, in 1813, when the collapse occurred, inflation was recorded as 311.2% (Abildgren 2010). Such a high inflation had not been observed before that date and throughout Denmark's history to date.

The rapid depreciation of the circulating courants, the efforts to finance the increasing expenditures by printing money, and the unsustainable trade made only the economic problems of the period. Besides, in addition to the political palace revolution, a king's heir who greedily mobilized all resources in order not to be on the losing side of the war ruled the state. In addition, Denmark lost Norway, which was very important to it, at the end of the war. As a result of all these political and economic developments, inflation rose rapidly, and the economy collapsed.

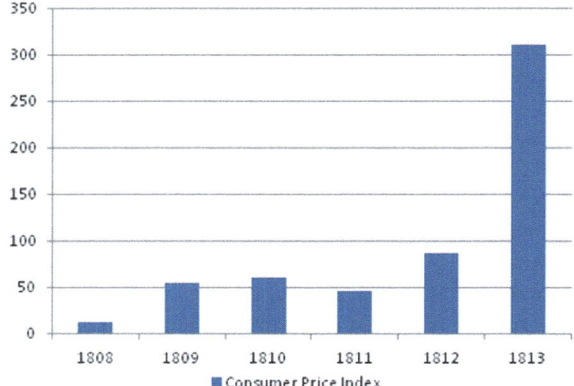

Chart 4.4 Consumer price index between 1808 and 1813. *Source* Abildgren (2010)

What made the bankruptcy of the Danish state so important was the financial reform announced on 5 January 1813. Considering developments such as the depreciation of courant banknotes due to the monetary expansion experienced and the nationalization of Kurantbank, which was established as a private bank, the necessity of financial reform is also clear.

In this regard, the financial reform had two important goals. The first is to reorganize and stabilize the monetary system, and the other is to resolve large amounts of unconvertible banknotes that are linked to the silver reserves in the market. To realize all these aims, Nationalbank was established in 1818, which held a monopoly of issuing banknotes to the market. The main goal of the Nationalbank until the 1830s was to achieve equality between banknotes and silver reserves. State-owned Riksbank was established in 1813 before the Nationalbank in order to ensure the unity of the money in circulation. The banknotes put into the market by Riksbank were classified as half, 1 and 2 riksdaler in terms of value for an easier use (Marcher 2012). However, another feature of Riksbank is that it collected mortgage deeds at the rate of 6% of the value of real estate in Denmark in order to ensure the trust in the bank. Because of this commitment, it was named as real estate bank. The property owners also agreed to pay an annual interest of 6.5% of the debt in exchange for using this mortgage value as pure silver if they wish (Abildgren 2018).

The circulation of different types of banknotes until 1813 made it difficult to achieve financial stability. Although the crisis was not felt much in the Duchies thanks to the banknotes used in the Duchies in 1788, the fact that their banknotes were in circulation was a contradiction for the monetary union. Using throughout the kingdom riksbankdaler, i.e., riksdaler, released by Riksbank was necessary in order to ensure monetary union. However, the use of this banknote was not welcomed in the Duchies, and therefore the Duchies were emancipated during the transition period.

Riksdaler banknotes released by Riksbank initially had difficulty in capturing the value of silver. In September 1813, the nominal value of riksdans remained 9% lower in terms of market value. Although the bank began withdrawing riksdalers in 1814, in the next few years riksdalers remained 30–40% below nominal value. This problem about the riksdaler caused the use of separate currency in the Duchies of Schleswig–Holstein in 1813 and ceding of Norway to Sweden with the agreement signed in Kiel in 1814. When Riksbank was established, the provision that the bank would be restructured as a private company was fulfilled in 1818 and Nationalbank was established (Abildgren 2009). Another important point here is that Riksbank put its real estate bank policy into practice in Nationalbank later and gave the right to buy stocks to people whose mortgage value is above a certain amount. Thus, the Nationalbank shareholders were made up of Danish property owners. Although the shareholders did not have a say in the management of the bank, dividend rights were granted. However, until 1845, Nationalbank did not pay dividends. The main reason for not giving shareholders a voice in management was to establish a bank that is independent not only from the state but also from shareholder interests (Abildgren 2018).

Riksbank was established by the government to ensure monetary union and stability. Considering the post-war period and the continuing high inflation, it is possible to say that the riksdaler was an optimistic try. However, with the peace agreement signed after the Napoleonic War, Norway's ceding to Sweden also negatively affected the trade. The loss of Norway, which is considered as a financially strong and commercially indispensable for Denmark, also contributed to the failure of riksdaler. On the other hand, Riksbank, which can be considered as a state intervention, was against Denmark's mercantilist identity. For this reason, it was stated that it would be restructured to operate as a joint stock company afterwards. Due to the failure of Riksdaler, it was considered more reasonable to close it completely and establish a new and private bank, Nationalbank.

Nationalbank was established to operate completely independent of the state. For this reason, it is stated in its corporation charter that it will be prevented from being affected by the state or from having a voice in its administration. In addition, the main purpose of its establishment was stated as to establish a secure monetary system. Thus, it was aimed to put banknotes into circulation with the loans provided to encourage trade and production (Andersen 2011). Thus, we can say that commercial activities intended to be re-established through Nationalbank were supported by loans.

4.5   Conclusion

During the seventeenth and eighteenth centuries, Denmark was a strong state with a strong trade and therefore economy with the facilities provided by the colonies. However, Norway had a special importance as it was the gateway to the north and the Baltic Sea. It is possible to say that there were also political frictions within the kingdom during the period in question. The belief that monetary stability cannot exist in economies dominated by political instability has once again been confirmed by Denmark. In this respect, the Crisis of 1813 is important. Even one can speculate, the independence of the Duchy of Schleswig–Holstein caused by the crisis with among other things (Sørensen 2013).

Increasing its defence expenditures to finance the public expenditures increasing due to the Seven Years' War and then the Napoleonic Wars and to survive in the war posed the main problem for Denmark like any other country in the aforesaid period. For this reason, the budget deficit increased in Denmark, as was the case for other countries. At this point, with the establishment of Kurantbank in Denmark, there was a conviction that the banknotes put on the market were an effective financing method. Although Kurantbank was established as a private bank, it could not survive because it released irreversible number of banknotes to the market due to its unlimited power to print money and reserves. In order for it to survive, it was expropriated with state support. Up to this point, it was deemed as a method for the government, which borrowed from the bank, to save on interest repayments and to print unlimited money. High inflation and the depreciation of the banknotes in circulation paved the way for the Duchies to establish their own banks first and to leave Denmark by adopting a different currency after the war.

The monetary stability which the country failed to achieve somehow, and high inflation revealed the necessity of monetary reform with the loss of the Napoleonic War. For this reason, financial reform was made on 5 January 1813. Within the scope of the financial reform, Riksbank was established by the government, and it was aimed to increase the use of riksdalers. However, the high inflation chronicled by the failure of the riksdalers to achieve the desired success and the ceding of Norway proved that a new method should have been adopted. For this reason, a completely private Nationalbank, which continues to operate today, was established.

References

Abildgren K (2006) Monetary trends and business cycles in Denmark 1875–2005: new evidence using the framework of financial accounts for organising historical financial statistics. Danmarks Nationalbank Working Papers No. 43. Danmarks Nationalbank, Copenhagen

Abildgren K (2009) Consumer prices in Denmark 1502–2007. Danmarks Nationalbank Working Papers No. 60. Danmarks Nationalbank, Copenhagen

Abildgren K (2010) Consumer price in Denmark 1502–2007. Scand Econ Hist Rev 58(1):2–24

Abildgren K (2018) Danmark Nationalbank 1818–2018. https://www.nationalbanken.dk/en/public ations/anniversary%20publications/Documents/Nationalbanken%201818-2018_uk.pdf

Andersen ES (2011) The evolution of Nordic finance. Springer

Bregnsbo M (2014) The motives behind the foreign political decisions of Frederick VI during the Napoleonic Wars. Scand J Hist 39(3):335–352

Colin J (1994) The Cambridge illustrated history of France. Cambridge University Press, New York, NY

Feldbaek O (2001) Denmark in the Napoleonic Wars: a foreign policy survey. Scand J Hist 26(2):89–101. https://doi.org/10.1080/034687501750211127

Götz N (2015) The Good Plumpuddings' belief: British voluntary aid to Sweden during the Napoleonic Wars. Int Hist Rev 37(3):519–539. https://doi.org/10.1080/07075332.2014.918559

Kagan F (2007) The end of the old order: Napoleon and Europe. Da Capo Press, Philadelphia

Marcher M (2012) Metals and reforms: a survey of Danish monetary history 1813–1873. In: Depreyrot G (ed) Moneys and economies during 19th century (from Europe to Asia): Proceedings of the round table of the 'silver monetary depreciation and international relations' program, Paris, pp 77–95

Marcher M, Talvio T, Heijne CV (ed) (2010) Danish banking before and after the Napoleonic Wars: a survey of Danish banking, 1736–1857. In: Monetary boundaries in transition: a north European economic history and the Finnish War 1808–1809, vol 16. Statens Historiska Museum Studies, pp 127–143

Ryan AN (1953) The causes of the British attack upon Copenhagen in 1807. Engl Hist Rev 68(266):37–55

Sørensen AR (2013) Monetary romanticism: nationalist rhetoric and monetary organisation in nineteenth century Denmark. Scand Econ Hist Rev 61(3):209–232

Thomas HA (2016) Historical dictionary of Denmark. Rowman & Littlefield Publishers, London

Winton P (2012) Sweden and the seven years war, 1757–1762: war, debt and politics. War Hist 19(1):5–31

Wullschlager J (2000) Hans Cristian Andersen: the life of a storyteller. The University of Chicago Press, Chicago

Yahil L (1991) National pride and defeat: a comparison of Danish and German nationalism. J Contemp Hist 26(3/4):453–478

Merve Dilara Boyner is a student of Ph.D. at the İzmir Katip Çelebi University at İzmir in Turkey. She is working on Financial Economics. Since she could get the title of Ph.D., she completed all process successfully. She received her bachelor's degree in economics from Erciyes University and her master's degree the department of public finance in Erciyes University. Her master's degree research is within the framework of international exchange of information and double taxation agreement Turkey-USA comparison.

Professor Dr. Bernur Açıkgöz was born in 1979 in Ankara. After attending Ankara Finance High School, she continued her undergraduate studies at Dokuz Eylül University, Department of Finance. She received her master's degree in Financial Law from Dokuz Eylül University. In 2006, she was awarded her Ph.D. degree from Dokuz Eylul University Department of Public Finance. Her Ph.D. thesis covered the topics of poverty and development.

In 2006, she won the Harvard University Project scholarship and worked as a visiting professor at Harvard University. In 2009, she received a scholarship from the Swiss Government for a post-doctorate degree in economics at the University of Neuchatel/Switzerland, and taught courses at Bern Universities. She then began to work in the fields of experimental economics and game theory, and for three consecutive years as a guest lecturer in the economics laboratory of the Montpellier University in Montpellier, France. Afterwards, she went to Missouri University, Indiana University and Arizona University with a scholarship from Missouri University. She then worked as a visiting professor at the University of East Anglia and took some courses from Exeter Universities in the UK with a Tubitak scholarship.

Professor Dr. Bernur Açıkgöz has books, articles and papers on foreign direct investments, economic growth, panel econometrics, experimental economics, and game theory. She is currently working at the Department of Public Finance and Financial Management at Izmir Katip Çelebi University/Turkey. In addition, Açıkgöz teaches at the Department of International Trade and Finance at Izmir University of Economics/Turkey and the Department of Economics at University of Life Sciences in Poznań (Uniwersytet Przyrodniczy w Poznaniu)/Poland.

Burhanettin Onur Kireçtepe is a research assistant at Tokat Gaziosmanpaşa University and a Ph.D. Candidate at Ankara Hacıbayramveli University in Turkey. He is working on Tax Law. His current research investigates the relationship between tax law and human rights. He received her bachelor's degree in law from Eastern Mediterranean University and his master's degree from the University of Aberdeen.

Chapter 5
1873–1896 Long Depression

Muhammet Kaya

Abstract The economic crisis of 1873–1896 is considered to be the first serious crisis that lasted for a long time on the international financial and trade system, which felt its effects in many countries and continents, albeit with different weights. The crisis consists of a series of financial crises that lasted from 1873 to 1896 but also included periods of recovery and decline during this period. The main feature of the period is the end of the "good years" period, which is attributed to the years 1846 to 1873, especially for England, and the unstoppable fall in product prices. In this period, while production and economic activities increased unsteadily, the price level tended to decrease with the same instability. Again, the said period includes the period when another crisis, the British agricultural crisis, was experienced in terms of the British agricultural sector. The most important result of the 1873–1896 crisis is considered to be the loss of the world industrial leadership, which England had maintained as a dominant power until the crisis, to Germany and the USA, which emerged as new industrial powers.

Keywords International financial and trade system · Long depression · Economic crises

5.1 Introduction

The economic crisis of 1873–1896, which was described as panic in its early periods and as "long depression" in later periods, is considered as the first serious crisis experienced by capitalism which long lasted on the international financial and trade system and which, contrary to the crisis and panics before it, made its effects felt in many countries and continents (Marichal 2009: 37–38; Rosenberg 1943: 59; Eğilmez 2012).

M. Kaya (✉)
Department of Public Finance and Financial Management, Graduate School of Social Sciences, Izmir Katip Celebi University, İzmir, Turkey
e-mail: mkaya3576@gmail.com

© The Author(s), under exclusive license to Springer Nature Singapore Pte Ltd. 2022   57
B. Açıkgöz (ed.), *Black Swan: Economic Crises, Volume I*, Accounting, Finance, Sustainability, Governance & Fraud: Theory and Application,
https://doi.org/10.1007/978-981-19-5252-4_5

The crisis consists of a series of financial crises that continued from 1873 to 1896, when cyclical fluctuations were experienced, including recovery in 1882 and 1890s and regression periods in 1879, 1886 and 1893. The main feature of the period is the unavoidable unstable decline in product prices with the end of the "good years" period attributed to the years 1846 to 1873, especially for the UK. However, it should be noted that there was no decline necessarily in economic and commercial activities in the said period. In this period, although production and trade volume continued to expand, the decreasing profitability rates due to price decreases increased investment concerns and negatively affected investment decisions in almost all areas (Musson 1959: 199–200; Rosenberg 1943: 59–60; Beales 1934: 68).

Although there are different opinions on the factors causing the crisis and its basic features, the period of 1873–1896, which is also characterized as the great depression, points out that the unstable tendency of production and economic activities to increase and the price level coincide with the steep downward trend with the same instability. Similarly, the failure of economic indicators such as interest and discount rates, commodity and stock prices, profit margins, nominal wages and saving tendency in this period to reach the level of good years reveals a separate feature of the period (Rosenberg 1943: 59–60).

The most important consequence of the 1873–1896 crisis is that the UK lost its industrial leadership of the world, which it had maintained as a dominant power until pre-crisis, to Germany and the USA, which emerged as new industrial powers (Aldcroft 1964: 116; Musson 1959: 208). The period in question also marks the period of another crisis for the agricultural sector in the UK, the Great Depression of British agriculture.

In the light of the explanations above, the explanations in the following sections will continue on the axis of the UK, which is considered to be the country most affected by the crisis, in a way to include the USA, Germany and the Great Depression of British agriculture that took place in this period.

5.1.1 Background of the Crisis

Some fundamental developments in the period until 1873 were associated with the crisis of 1873–1896 by most authors. Some of these developments are the end of the civil war in the USA, the Prussian-Austrian war of 1866, the re-collapse of Overend, Gurney and Company in 1866, the "Wunderharvest" phenomenon in Austrian wheat that gave a fresh impetus to Austrian railway traffic and exports in 1867, when Europe encountered scarce crops, the opening of the Suez Channel in 1869, the unpredictable success of the Their leases published in 1871 and 1872, the Chicago fire of October 1871, the relaxation of German banking laws, the Crédit Mobilier scandal in financing the Erie and Union Pacific railways, and the Granger movement in the West (Kindleberger 1990: 312).

Although it is associated with many events before 1873, the beginning of the crisis was the panic that occurred in a bank in Vienna on 8 May 1873, and the subsequent collapse of the Vienna stock market that led to a three-day closure. The phenomenon, which was initially ignored, seemed limited only to Austria-Hungary and described as panic, turned into a system crisis with a knock-on effect in a short time and spread to European financial companies and from here to the USA. The first effect of the crisis that would continue until 1896 with the periods of decline and recovery caused turmoil in the capital markets of the nations investing in the US railways sector and thus the sector suffered serious losses. The said process, which caused the suspension of the railway projects, which was the driving force of the period economy in the United States, caused a five-year recession in the country. The financial crisis also led to a global decline in international trade, with the domino effect, and various debt crises in many countries, including the Ottoman Empire and Latin American countries (Wikipedia 2020a, b; Marichal 2009: 37–38).

The spread of the crisis to Europe and the USA in a short time and the fact that it was widespread and intense enough to affect many countries is explained by the fact that two dominant money markets, namely the London and Paris money markets, which were considered the two dominant money markets in the world financial system until the 1870s, gave way to interconnected primary and secondary financial centres. Therefore, the crisis of 1873 is considered as a process triggered by financial difficulties in Central Europe and the USA rather than a crisis triggered by these two dominant financial centres, unlike the financial crises experienced before (Marichal 2009: 37–38).

However, according to Kindleberger, the links between financial markets and macroeconomics are not only related to money flow, but also to commodities and securities subject to foreign trade. Therefore, the ups and downs of an economy can also be spread by the psychological reactions that arise in the change of commercial relations between the two countries (Kindleberger 1990: 312).

In this context, it is inevitable that a problem in the American railways' system directly affects the European financial system and the problems in the European development sector mutually affect the American financial system, in such a situation which is described as "asymmetric information" and expresses the mutual fragility of the European and the US economies, which have tight financial and trade ties with each other (Akbaş 2017; 85–86).

It is even claimed that the compensation paid caused the 1914 World War in the following processes. Another approach to explain the reason why the crisis affected the USA is the tight monetary policies followed in the country on the basis of gold monetary policy after the US civil war. In this period, the scarcity of gold, which determined the value of money, was a determinant in shaping the process (Eğilmez 2012). Germany, which completed its political union in 1871, switched to a gold money standard after America abandoned the use of silver money and switched to gold-based pricing, which is among the factors that contribute to the process in question (Balı and Büyükşalvarcı 2011: 66–69).

In this period, it is observed that countries such as Germany, the US and Italy entered a rapid industrialization process by ensuring their national unions, and large development projects were implemented at an increasing speed in Europe's big cities such as Paris, Berlin and Vienna. With the contribution of factors such as; development projects using mortgage loans, efficient production in the US in the agriculture and husbandry sector, the advances in sea transportation resulting in reducing freight prices, and especially the UK's persistent avoidance of protectionist approach in agriculture, etc., the weakening in the European agricultural sector in the process and the loss of income due to this weakening caused these sectors in Europe had hard times, making the repayment of the loans used in this field difficult. The negative developments in the agricultural sector, which put the financial systems into trouble regarding the loan repayments, spread to the European real estate market over time. Upon these developments, the closure of the financial faucets of the British financial companies against Europe brought the crisis to the US economy, where there is a heavy investment in its railways (Marichal 2009: 38–39; Akbaş 2017: 86).

As stated above, the factors that triggered the 1873 crisis are not solely due to the decline in commodity prices and the problems in the US railways industry. The £200 million war reparations France had to pay in the aftermath of the Franco-Prussian war caused a large capital flow from London and Paris markets to the Central European economies and therefore investment booms, especially in Germany, while on the other hand, it made Western European financial markets unstable, and also brought along a cycle that spread to the unindustrialized regions of the Near East and Latin America in the form of a debt crisis (Balı and Büyükşalvarcı 2011: 68; Marichal 2009: 39).

On the other hand, in general, it is also claimed that during the crisis of 1873–1896 when the production level was maintained despite the general level of prices decreased, there were positive results in terms of prices and real wages for consumers and employees in the long run, and in this sense, the crisis had a positive contribution to the redistribution of income, and there is no uninterrupted series of bad years for the producers and investors (Rosenberg 1943: 61).

5.1.2   The United States

Contemporary authors and theorists argue that the economic disasters of the 1870s were shaped around two main factors. In this context, some authors argue that the main factor underlying the collapse is the global decline in commodity prices, while others argue that the crisis is associated with the stagnation in the railway sector, the strongest and most international economic activity of the period (Marichal 2009: 38).

Following the end of the civil war, the United States of America (USA) made progress that can be considered economically significant between 1868 and 1873. The most important driving force of these developments was seen as the serious steps taken in the railway sector. In this period, which is considered as "good years" all over the world, especially in the UK, while the production of physical goods increased steadily in the USA, significant developments were achieved with the restructuring of the agricultural sector in the South. With the effect of the almost doubling of the railway network, both the agricultural exports and the number of immigrants increased (Wells 1937: 238).

Again, while productivity per worker in agriculture increased faster than manufacturing in this period, the rise of railways and steamships in the United States in the 1870s considerably reduced the transportation costs, so up to 25% was saved in the freight rates in exports from the USA to the UK. The Homestaed Law, adopted in the USA in 1862, enabled the settlement in the middle parts of the continent, and the acceleration of investments in new railway networks paved the way for the increase in domestic transportation possibilities and the development of farming with new inventions in agricultural machinery (Wikipedia 2020a, b; Musson 1959: 218).

In the aftermath of the US civil war, more than 90,000 km of new railroads were constructed in the US across the country between 1866 and 1873, especially with the effect of land donations and cash aid provided by the government (Balı and Büyükşalvarcı 2011: 66). In the same period, more than 20,000 miles of railroads were built in Russia (Marichal 2009: 38). According to Kaymak's citation from Ashworth, the railway investments made by British companies in many countries of the world, especially in North USA, from 1840s had a great effect on the said development. The railway line in the world, which was 7.679 km in 1840, increased to 209.795 km in 1873.

Especially the acceleration experienced in the railway sector resulted in the intense interest of speculators in a short time, governments and individuals borrowed money to finance almost all enterprises, especially railway construction, and large sums were paid to large projects with no return in a short time (Wells 1937: 238).

On the other hand, the USA, which changed its silver policy with the Coin Law of 1873, adopted the gold currency standard and gave up purchasing silver and printing silver coins at the officially determined price. After this decision of the USA, which gave up silver with the adopted gold currency standard, silver prices fell rapidly to affect western miners, and interest rates increased as a result of the decrease in the domestic money supply due to the shortage of gold. The increase in interest rates in this cycle caused farmers and those with especially large debts have a hard time paying their debts (Balı and Büyükşalvarcı 2011: 66).

Due to financial excesses and speculative investments, by the middle of the summer of 1873, the momentum that the USA provided in its economy after the civil war suddenly stopped. Because the railway system, which reached saturation in the flotation of new securities, grew excessively and unnecessarily. The first effects of the fear caused by the panic atmosphere were the fall in stock and commodity prices, the default of bonds, the failure of over-expanded banks and the contraction of loans (Wells 1937: 238–240).

According to Mishkin, the first disturbance in the process is due to financial problems in the railway sector. The suspension of operations of the Missouri, Kansas, and Texas Railways, as well as the New York Warehouse & Security Company, which also gave substantial loans to grain and products, on 8 September 1873, was followed by Kenyon, Cox & Co. Banking's failure. The severity of the situation was realized when the developments, which were thought to be insignificant at first, were followed by the suspension of Jay Cooke & Co., one of the most respected and important financial institutions in the US, on 18 September and the suspension of Fisk & Hatch following day. The collapse of Jay Cooke & Co. was also due to financial difficulties in the rail sector, particularly problems with loans it made to the North Pacific Railway, which Jay Cooke & Co. controlled. Failing to sell its North Pacific Railway Bills during this period, the shortage in the money supply caused by the gold currency standard and the decrease in loan returns due to high-interest rates combined, caused Jay Cooke & Company to go bankrupt in a short time. Jay Cooke & Co. With the announcement of its failure, the stock market had a selling trend. When H. Clews Bank went bankrupt after Cooke, other banks in the country also started to go bankrupt and the New York Stock Exchange was temporarily closed for 10 days. 18 September 1873 was named as "Black Thursday", when the decrease in stock prices exceeded %7 in September (Balı and Büyükşalvarcı 2011: 66–67; Mishkin 1991: 80–81).

These negative developments brought about the decrease in nominal wages, the unfinished construction and the melting of company profits. Railways unions carried out a major strike in 1877, as workers dismissed from factories increased. These developments have paved the way for the emergence of some social unrest. The events that took place created a wave of internal migration in the country that would last until the end of the 1920s. According to citations made by Balı and Büyükşalvarcı from Rezneck, 89 out of 364 railway companies went bankrupt between 1873 and 1879. In just two years since the onset of the crisis, 18,000 workplaces went bankrupt and the unemployment rate reached 14% in this period (Balı and Büyükşalvarcı 2011: 67–68).

However, according to Wells, while agricultural prices decreased by 30% in the period of 1873–1879, agricultural production increased by 50%. The current land compatible with the rapidly increasing population, the expansion of railways to the west and the rapid expansion in the agricultural area brought by the new agricultural machinery were effective in this increase. Non-agricultural prices, on the other hand, declined slightly over 35% in the period when prices reached their lowest level. However, although both agricultural and non-agricultural prices tended to fall from 1873 to 1879, according to Wells, trade, industry and agriculture in the USA were not in the crisis (Wells 1937: 240–243).

5.1.3 Germany-Austria

Germany, which achieved its union with Bismarck in 1871, made significant economic progress in many areas, especially in steel production and railway construction. Such that Germany surpassed France with this momentum and by 1914 became the most important industrial rival for the USA. With the political union, the obstacles to economic growth were removed, the gold-based currency was adopted and the imperial central bank started operation. On the other hand, thanks to the removal of obstacles that complicate setting up a company, 857 new companies were established between 1871 and 1873 with a total capital of 1.4 million taler (silver money). All these regulations, together with the said war indemnity, brought an unprecedented growth-oriented change to the German economy between the years 1870 and 1873, which are called "Gründerjahre" or "Year of Establishments". Again, in the country where the railway network doubled between 1865 and 1875, the investments in stocks in the railway system also increased during this period (Britannica 2020).

War reparations incomes received by Germany from France after the France-Prussia war were used in domestic and foreign debt payments. The redemption of German government bonds, estimated to be held in Austria, amounting to 1 billion marks, led to an investment boom in Austrian railways, and between 1864 and 1867, the railway system expanded 16% per kilometre and 38% in traffic, especially, as a result of "Wunderharvest" (miracle harvest). On the other hand, this redemption led to the start of a new investment glut for Austrian investors from iron, steel and railway vehicles to other related sectors, and the expansion of financial institutions consisting of banks and broker banks lending to buyers of securities (Kinderberger 1990: 313).

On the other hand, the establishment of Berlin as the capital city increased the immigration to the city and led to the arrival of banks originated in other locations, in time. Again, in the financing of foreign trade of Germany, new types of banking, called Baubanken or construction banks, were formed in addition to mixed banks such as Deutsche Bank, which was established in 1872 to compete with London. According to Kinderberger, these were buildings that were ostensibly financed by banks, but in reality, it was nothing more than speculation financed on construction sites (Kinderberger 1990: 313–314).

The financial crisis, which started with the collapse of the Vienna stock market that ignited the crisis of 1873, soon affected Germany. Since the process that caused the decrease in the prices of agricultural and industrial products in the first place had a direct effect on the profitability of the company, there was a sharp decrease in investments and 20% of the recently established companies were driven into bankruptcy. Among the companies that went bankrupt was Bethel Henry Strousberg, the pioneer of German railways. According to what Kaymak cites from Beaud, and iron prices decreased by 37% as the iron consumption decreased by 50% in Germany in 1873–1877 due to the impact of the crisis. In the collapse process called "Gründerkrach" or "The Collapse of the Institutions", in which the war reparations payments by France ended, the German economy shrank significantly (Britannica 2020; Balı and Büyükşalvarcı 2011: 68–69).

5.1.4 The United Kingdom

The UK is considered to be the country where the crisis of 1873–1896 was felt most intensely. With its economic development process that started in the 1850s and reached its highest level in 1872, the UK was the dominant power of the period in terms of investment, capital export and export as well as industry. Such that exports increased from £97 million to £256 million in 1854, while imports increased from

£152 million to £355 million and re-exports from £19 million to £58 million. On the other hand, coal production, cotton consumption, pig-iron production, transportation and shipbuilding figures were uncompetitive. British traders and investors acted as contractors, franchisees and financiers in almost every corner of the world, primarily in railway and development works. However, the growth, which peaked in 1872, was replaced by a decline as of 1873. During the period of 1873–1896, a recession that lasted until 1879 was followed by a recovery period that lasted for three years, followed by a four-year recession and recovery in 1882–1886, and after a severe depression in 1890–1896, prices recovered and the depression came to an end (Beales 1934: 65–71).

The main feature of the period is the persistent decline in product prices. For the UK, the reasons for the price decrease of up to 40% are overproduction, gold appreciation due to gold shortage, withdrawal of silver from the market, protectionist tariffs in foreign trade, speculative movements, bad harvest periods, failure of foreign debt and foreign investments to create sufficient foreign demand for British goods (Musson 1959: 202–205).

However, as stated before, although the price level decreased, data that would reveal the contraction in economic growth were not available in this period. On the contrary, almost all economic activity indexes (coal and pig iron production, tonnage of constructed ships, raw wool and cotton consumption, foreign trade figures, shipping entries and cargoes, passenger traffic, bank deposits and permits, joint stock company formations, trade profits, food consumption etc.) had an upward trend (Musson 1959: 199–200).

On the other hand, it was argued that price decreases mainly affected industrialists, traders and financiers in terms of profitability and interest rates. Again, while real wages increased significantly during this period, positive developments were experienced regarding the position of the working class, and a redistribution of national income in favour of wage earners was witnessed. Again in this period, while poverty decreased, per capita consumption of foodstuffs, beer, tobacco products and similar products increased, and deposits in savings banks grew steadily (Musson 1959: 200–206).

Chart 5.1 shows the UK's wholesale price index for the period 1815–1913. It is clear in the aforementioned chart that the prices peaked in 1873 in the period between 1840 and 1873, and then had a downward trend.

The wholesale price indices for some product groups in the period between 1871 and 1895 are given in Table 5.1. It is stated, in the analysis made on the basis of products, that the price of sugar and oil decreased the most while the price of animal products such as milk, egg, butter and meat decreased the least.

As can be understood from the aforementioned data and explanations, it is seen that animal food prices were relatively maintained compared to other products. Saul explains this by the fact that people spend their income more on animal products such as milk, eggs, butter and meat as the prices of other products fall and the standard of living rises due to the increase in income, and the income elasticity of demand. On the other hand, the low price of sugar beet and oil compared to other products is

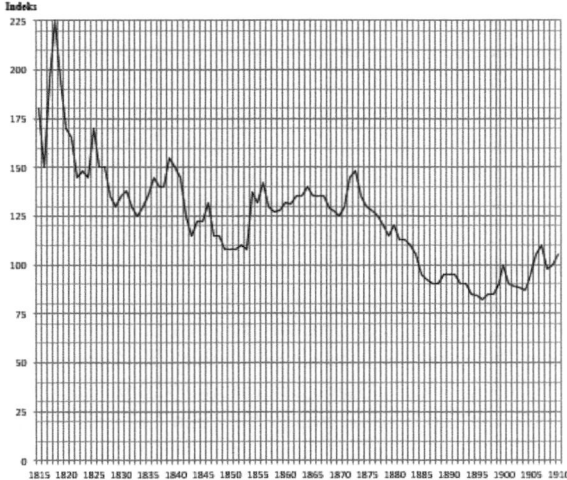

Chart 5.1   Wholesale prices in Britain, 1815–1910, (1900 = 100)

Table 5.1   Board of trade wholesale price indices (1871–5 = 100)

	Coal and metals	Textile fibres	Grains	Animal products	Sugar, tea, tobacco, coffee and cocoa	Total index
1871–5	100	100	100	100	100	100
1876–80	66.7	85.4	95.4	102.6	90.2	92
1881–5	60.7	76.9	83.7	98.6	75.1	83.5
1886–90	61.5	66.5	67.7	84.8	56.8	70.6
1891–5	63.6	60.3	66	84.6	53.7	68.3

justified by the subsidies given in Europe for sugar beet and the opening of new oil wells.

As stated before, different reasons have been put forward in various studies to reveal the reason for price decreases. Among these, explanations based on the quantity theory of money were not widely accepted in the face of the realities of the increase in bank deposits and gold reserves and the decline in interest rates in the period in question, again, the effect of the return of productive investments before 1873, including overseas countries, technological developments constantly reducing the cost, the improvements in land and sea transportation and the efficiency achieved in transportation with the opening of the Suez Canal are among these reasons. For example, in a calculation made on freight, it was revealed that unit cost of transporting Baltic Fir Timber to London was 30.4 cents in 1863, and decreased to 14 cents in 1884, while unit cost of transporting Black Sea wheat to Liverpool costed 17.9 cents on a unit basis in 1864, while this figure decreased to 8.8 cents in 1886. Another reason for the price decline is that the UK industry, which was the dominant power in world trade and even had a 30% share in the world primary product trade between 1867 and 1870, began to slow down and the input demand for industrial production, which slowed down thereby, was negatively affected (Musson 1959: 202–205).

Decreasing product prices naturally affected the profitability rates of the company, and this caused negative perceptions in business life and thus, investment and productivity. Despite the decrease in prices, production increased, albeit with a low rate of increase. The annual growth rate, which was 3–4% in the 1870s, then fell below 2%, and the industrial productivity rate, which was over 2% in the 1850s and 1860s, fell below 1% in later periods. The annual growth rate in manufacturing industry production between 1873 and 1913 was 1.8% in the UK, 4.8% in the USA, 3.9% in Germany and 3.7% in the world. Although the industrial productivity rate increased by 1.6% in the USA and 2.6% in Germany between 1873 and 1883, it progressed very slowly in the UK. The UK clearly lost its industrial leadership towards the end of the century (Musson 1959: 205–208).

The slowdown in the UK's industry since 1873 has been justified for many reasons. With the expansion of industrial production outside of the UK, the superiority achieved by the UK in industry since the 1840s passed to the newly industrialized USA and Germany as of 1873. The reasons for the decrease in production efficiency especially in iron and steel, coal and cotton weaving sectors are, unlike Germany and the USA, the fact that the old and cumbersome factories causing cost increase in iron-steel sector are lack of new technology, are not modernized and new processes cannot be developed in production processes, increasing depths in coal production, difficulties due to geological conditions and inadequacy in the use of technical equipment in the weaving sector and inability to develop new industries such as chemical engineering (Musson 1959: 206–208).

The data on the iron and steel production of the UK, Germany and the USA in the period of 1880–1913, which supports the mentioned points, are given in Table 5.2. From the aforementioned data, it is clearly seen that the UK left its leadership in the production of the said products to Germany and the USA.

Table 5.2 UK, Germany, USA iron and steel production, 1880–1913 (mil./ton)

	1880	1913
Iron		
U.K.	7.7	10.3
Germany	2.5	19.3
U.S.A.	3.8	31.0
Steel		
U.K.	1.3	7.7
Germany	0.7	18.9
U.S.A.	1.2	31.3

As was the case for iron and steel, the UK lost the leadership in coal production to the USA and Germany. British coal production, which was 31.8% in 1870, decreased to 19.5% in 1896–1900, while the coal production in the USA increased from 23.3% to 30.1%, and in Germany from 13.2 to 16.6% (Musson 1959: 208–209).

Among the other factors that led to the decline in the UK industrial productivity and production increase and Germany and the USA to gain superiority over the UK, despite the intense protectionism understanding developed in foreign trade during this period, the persistence of free trade policy and evaluating the capital abroad with the purpose of providing more returns instead of using capital in efficient investment areas (Musson 1959: 210).

When the data in Table 5.3 regarding the net domestic capital formation rates in the UK, Germany and the USA in the period of 1855–1914 are examined, it is seen that the UK is in a very disadvantaged position compared to its potential rivals in this field.

Declining industrial investments and decreasing industrial productivity of the UK due to the reasons mentioned above naturally had a negative impact on the foreign trade data of the country. However, the decline in UK exports made a positive contribution to the increase in the production and productivity of Germany and the USA (Musson 1959: 210). Although this is the case, it should be noted that the share of foreign trade in national income peaked at 29.5% in the 1870s and 1880s (Saul 1965: 5).

The distribution of the UK foreign capital investments by sectors is given in Table 5.4. The share of railway investments in these investments is around 40%. However, according to Pollard, some part of this share was financed indirectly by loans to foreign governments. While capital export constituted an average of 5% of GDP in the early periods, it increased to 7% in 1905–1913 and almost 9% in 1911–13. On the other hand, income from foreign capital investments increased from approximately 5% of GDP in the early 1870s to 9–10% in 1910–14 and more than a quarter of all real estate revenues (Pollard 1985: 490–491).

Between 1871 and 1913, the saving rate is around 11–15% of GDP in the UK, the USA and Germany. On the other hand, although domestic investment is around 12% in Germany and the USA, it corresponds to only 7% of GDP in the UK. This leads to the assumption that the remainder of the savings, in other words, a considerable amount of capital is sent out of the country. In the light of the aforementioned explanations, capital export emerges as an important debate issue in the justifications regarding the slowdown and land loss for the UK. It is deemed that British capital

Table 5.3 Net domestic capital formation as a percentage of net domestic product

U.K.		Germany		U.S.A.	
1855–74	**7.0**	1851–70	**8.5**	1869–80	**13.9**
1875–94	**6.8**	1871–90	**11.4**	1889–1913	**12.9**
1895–1914	**7.7**	1891–1913	**15.0**		

Table 5.4 Percentage distribution of New British Abroad

	1865–72	1909–1913
Agriculture	1.7	5.6
Minning	5.2	9.3
Manufacture	0.7	4.8
Transportation	47.6	46.6
Utilities	5.5	6.4
Public works	17.8	17.3
Other, including defence	21.5	10.0
	100	100

Source Pollard (1985: 490)

assets abroad, which were about £1,000–£1,200 (£ million) in 1875, rose by £4,000 (£ million) until the First World War (Pollard 1985: 489–490).

On the other hand, regarding the export data of the 1850–1873 period; although the country's average export, which was 116 million pounds annually in the 1855–1859 period, increased to 235 million pounds in the 1870–1874 period, which could not be exceeded until the period 1895–1899. For the period of 1873–1896, the lowest value which was 192 million pounds in 1879 reached a high value at 263 million pounds in 1890. While the annual average export volume was 5.3% annually between 1840 and 1860, it was 4.4% between 1860 and 1870, 2.1% in the 1870–1890 period and 0.7% in the 1890–1900 period. Considering the import data for the same period, imports, which was 146 million pounds annually in the 1855–1859 period, increased to 291 million pounds in the 1870–1874 period. The import volume was 4.5% between 1840 and 1860, while it was 4.4% in the 1860–1870 period, 2.9% between 1870 and 1890 and 2.6% in the 1890–1900 period (Musson 1959: 213–214).

When Table 5.5 data regarding the export data of the main developed countries in the period of 1870–1899 are examined, it is observed that the exports of Germany and the USA are in an increasing trend compared to the UK (Beales 1934: 73).

The difference between the mentioned import and export figures of the UK naturally caused an increase in the foreign trade deficit. The foreign trade deficit, which

Table 5.5 U.K., Germany, USA and France's 1870–1899 export data-annual, £ million

Average	UK	Germany	USA	France
1870–4	235	114 (1872–4)	96	135
1875–9	202	132	125	138
1880–4	234	153	165	138
1885–9	226	151	146	132
1890–4	234	153	185	137
1895–9	238	181	213	144

Source Beales (1934: 73)

Table 5.6 Wages in The U.K., 1868–1886 [1900 = 100]

	Nominal wages	Retail prices	Real wages	Consumption index	Total wage payments
1868	72.6	133.7	60.1	66.0	47.9
1873	86.6	137.1	69.9	77.0	68.3
1879	81.6	115.7	74.9	74.3	60.6
1883	83.2	114.6	76.0	78.9	66.2
1886	82.7	103.4	82.5	76.3	62.0
1870–5 (avg.)	86.6	130.8	68.9	73.8	61.4
1880–5 (avg.)	82.7	115.3	76.2	76.9	64.0

was 62.5 million pounds annually in the 1871–1875 period, increased to 130.3 million pounds in 1891–1895. In addition, the foreign investment recovered after 1875 and the capital export, which was 1069.3 million pounds, doubled to 2192.2 million pounds in 1895, and the return from this increase contributed to the closing of the foreign trade deficit (Musson 1959: 214–215).

Despite the persistent fall in product prices and the decline in economic growth, nominal wages declined more moderately with the development of organized unionism. Despite the decrease in nominal wages, the increase in real wages is explained by the increase in purchasing power due to the decrease in product prices. Table 5.6 includes wage data for the period 1868–1886.

Unemployment rates were 5.03% in the 1850–1859 period, 5.16% in the 1860–1870 period, 3.83% in the 1870–1879 period, 5.61% in the 1880–1889 period and 4.35% in the 1890–1899 period. It is considered that the continuation of production or economic growth, despite the decrease in prices, prevented unemployment rates from reaching high levels.

5.2 The Great Depression of British Agriculture (1873–1896)

The depression of 1873–1896 mainly heavily affected the agricultural sector in the UK. When the stubborn decline in prices coincided with the bad harvest periods in the last period of the 1870s, the effects of the crisis began to be felt more deeply and intensely, especially for wheat producers.

The main characteristics of the period in the agricultural sector in the UK can be summarized as the sharp decrease in wheat prices, increase in imports and decrease in arable agricultural land. However, it is concluded that although arable agricultural areas decreased, increasing animal production balanced this decrease and consequently agricultural production did not decrease (Musson 1959: 226).

The leadership of the UK in the field of industry in the period of 1846–1873 brought the soil to the second plan in this period and the capital directed to foreign financial markets through investment goods with higher returns. The thought that the source of wealth was industrial production instead of land, which emerged in time among the landowners, was also effective in this. For this reason, Kaynak explains the reason why protectionist discourses were put into the backburner even during the depression period, with the higher non-agricultural trade industry and financial returns of large landowners.

On the other hand, as can be seen from the data in Table 5.7 regarding the distribution of labor force in the UK for the period of 1841–1911, as a result of puting the agriculture into the backburner, agricultural employment also tends to relatively decrease continuously. The sectors that support the relative increase in employment especially before 1891 are as trade and transportation (Ashworth 1965: 62).

According to Musson, no other country in overseas trade was in a dangerous economic impasse like the UK. According to him, the UK sacrificed its agriculture to industry and trade. As stated, the UK exports a significant portion of its manufacturing due to its policy in foreign trade and imported raw materials and food products in return. However, the industrial competition to which it is increasingly exposed in foreign trade has forced the UK to pay less for food products. On the other hand, the fact that the agricultural population of Germany and the USA, which are the main industrial rivals, constitute a large part of the total population, and British agriculture, which was suppressed by falling freight prices due to the developing agriculture and transportation facilities in these countries, increased foreign dependency in this regard (Musson 1959: 225).

Especially with The Corn Laws abolished in 1846, customs duties on imported grains were also terminated, and a free policy was preferred in foreign trade and this policy was persistently pursued. Thus, the exports of foreign competitors to the UK increased steadily. Imports of finished and semi-finished products to the UK were 18.4% and 64.5 million pounds annually in 1870–1875 and increased to 24% and 100.4 million pounds in 1890–1895 (Musson 1959: 227; Gourevitch 1977: 282).

Table 5.7 Distribution of the labour force of Great Britain, 1841–1911 (percentages of total occupied population)

	Agriculture, forestry, fishing	Manufacture, minning, building	Trade and transport	Domestic and personal service	Public services, professions and all others
1841	22.2	40.5	14.2	14.5	8.5
1851	21.7	42.9	15.8	13.0	6.7
1861	18.7	43.6	16.6	14.3	6.9
1871	15.1	43.1	19.6	15.3	6.8
1881	12.6	43.5	21.3	15.4	7.3
1891	10.5	43.9	22.6	15.8	7.1
1901	8.7	46.3	21.4	14.1	9.6
1911	8.3	46.4	21.5	13.9	9.9

Source Ashworth (1965: 62)

Table 5.8 Tariff Levels in Industry and Agriculture

	High Tariff on Industry	Low Tariff on Industry
High Tariff on Agriculture	France, Germany, Italy	Austria-Hungary
Low Tariff on Agriculture	Australia, United States, Canada	Great Britain, Argentina

Source Gourevitch (1977: 282)

Table 5.8 which includes the data of countries applying low and high tariffs in terms of industry and agriculture sectors in 1873 shows that the USA and Germany were turning to protection walls in foreign trade, whereas the UK preferred a relatively free policy in this area (Gourevitch 1977: 282).

With the crisis that started in 1873, while many countries built their foreign trade with protection walls, the UK did not give up this choice. Falling freight prices due to the rise of steamships allowed US agricultural products to enter the UK much cheaper. Because the UK was the only industrialized country of the period that did not impose tariffs on industrial and agricultural products. The UK, which did not need tariffs thanks to its developed industry during the good years, provided additional financing and organization to the stock market by providing cheap food in exchange for developed industrial products from the world. However, this started to change after 1873. While the UK has entered into a continuous industrial decline since this date, the USA and Germany have emerged as new industrial powers. Other countries began to use their own products instead of British goods, to compete with the UK in foreign markets, to enter the British domestic market and to apply tariffs against British goods (Gourevitch 1977: 297).

In this period, productivity in the agricultural sector increased less than the productivity in the industrial sector. While the productivity increase was 15% between 1867–1869 and 1886–1893, this rate was 23% in the industrial sector. The share of income obtained from agriculture in the net national income decreased from 20% in the period 1855–1859 to 13% in the period 1870–1874 and to 6% in the period 1895–1899.

When Table 5.9 data, which includes the distribution of British agricultural products in 1870, 1895 and 1910 on a product basis derived from the studies of Bellerby and Dewey by Turner, is examined, agricultural crops accounted for half of the total agricultural products before the crisis and decreased to one third by the 1910s. The most dramatic decrease, on the basis of products, is observed in wheat and barley; and animal products, especially milk, dairy products and eggs, as well as cattle and pig production increased significantly (Turner 1992: 45).

Examining Table 5.10, compiled by Hunt and Pam using various studies and which includes the index numbers of the annual prices of wheat, barley, oats, pork, mutton, wool, beef, milk, butter and cheese between 1873 and 1898, is examined; in general, it is understood that the decrease in agricultural product prices was more than that of animal products, on the other hand, the most remarkable price decrease

Table 5.9 Product distribution in UK agriculture

	1870 (1)	1895 (2)	1910 (3)	1909/13 (4)	1909 (5)
	(In percentage)				
Crops					
Wheat	12.7	2.3	4.5	5.2	4.0
Barley	7.9	4.5	3.5	4.1	2.5
Oats	4.3	3.5	3.7	4.1	3.5
Rye	0.01	0.01	0.01		
Potatoes	7.3	7.2	4.7		
Hay	6.2	9.4	7.6	} 5.7	} 7.1
Straw	4.6	2.5	2.0	} 9.2	} 11.5
Vegetables	1.6	3.0	3.6		
Fruits	0.5	1.7	3.0		
Hops	1.2	1.2	0.9		
Flax	0.9	0.2	0.2		
	47.2	**35.5**	**33.7**	**28.3**	**28.6**
Livestock					
Catle	10.9	13.8	17.0	17.4	20.2
Sheep	6.3	6.9	7.1	7.3	12.2
Wool	4.1	3.4	2.8	2.9	2.9
Pigs	8.1	13.9	4.4	8.5	11.4
Milk and its products	19.2	19.4	26.4	28.0	18.0
Eggs	2.0	3.7	5.0		
Poultry	0.7	1.3	2.0	} 7.5	} 6.7
Horses	1.5	2.1	1.8		
	52.8	**64.5**	**66.5**	**71.6**	**71.4**

Source Turner (1992: 46)

was experienced in wheat and wool products, and at the end of the period, especially the prices of wool hit the bottom, whereas the price drops of food of animal origin such as meat, milk, oil and cheese remained shallow or relative compared to other products.

Based on the aforementioned price index, the price index chart for the UK regarding wheat, barley and oat products for the period of 1873–1898 is shown in Chart 5.1. As can be seen from the aforementioned chart, the decrease in wheat prices in the mentioned period was greater during the period compared to barley and oats (Chart 5.2).

Although wheat prices decreased during the crisis, the ratio of wheat crop to gross product was 13% in the period of 1867–1876 which decreased to 4% in the

Table 5.10   Farm price indices, 1873–1898 (1871–5 = 100)

	Wheat	Barley	Oats	Pork	Mutton	Wool	Beef	Milk	Butter	Cheese
1873	107	102	97	102	107	109	105	100	99	101
1874	102	111	110	102	90	93	96	104	104	94
1875	83	97	109	107	100	88	103	107	101	95
1876	84	89	100	111	98	79	97	104	107	93
1877	104	101	99	96	92	73	92	100	100	105
1878	85	102	93	94	93	67	92	100	94	91
1879	80	86	83	90	88	56	84	100	93	80
1880	81	84	88	103	92	68	92	96	91	100
1881	83	81	83	102	97	55	90	100	91	91
1882	82	79	83	96	102	50	96	100	92	93
1883	76	81	82	92	103	45	96	100	95	96
1884	65	78	77	90	90	45	92	93	94	93
1885	60	76	78	85	80	44	82	93	91	100
1886	57	67	72	85	85	45	75	86	80	82
1887	59	64	62	81	71	47	67	89	82	91
1888	58	71	64	75	80	46	73	89	81	86
1889	54	65	68	81	85	49	73	89	83	83
1890	58	73	71	79	76	49	71	89	82	80
1891	68	71	76	73	71	44	75	86	86	79
1892	55	66	76	90	71	39	71	86	84	77
1893	48	65	71	94	71	46	73	93	80	75
1894	42	62	65	83	71	45	69	86	77	75
1895	42	56	55	70	75	54	69	79	72	66
1896	48	58	56	66	66	51	64	79	75	56
1897	55	60	64	83	69	43	67	79	72	72
1898	62	69	70	85	63	39	67	79	72	60

Source Hunt and Pam (2002: 480)

period 1894–1903. It was suggested that the changing demand structure over time encouraged British farmers to produce meat and milk instead of potatoes and wheat (Fletcher 1961: 417–418).

Chart 5.3, where the dramatic decline in wool prices is exhibited, reveals that the wool prices, which started to decrease since the 1860s, collapsed after a short recovery in the period of 1871–1875.

The chart displaying wheat production and wheat production areas in the period of 1852–1890 is given in Charts 5.3 and 5.4. From the aforementioned chart, it is observed that wheat production and cultivated areas shrank significantly during the depression period (NBER 2020).

Chart 5.2 UK wheat, barley and oat prices (wheat, barley and oat, 1871–5 = 100). *Source* Derived from the 1873–1898 agricultural price index (Hunt and Pam 2002: 480)

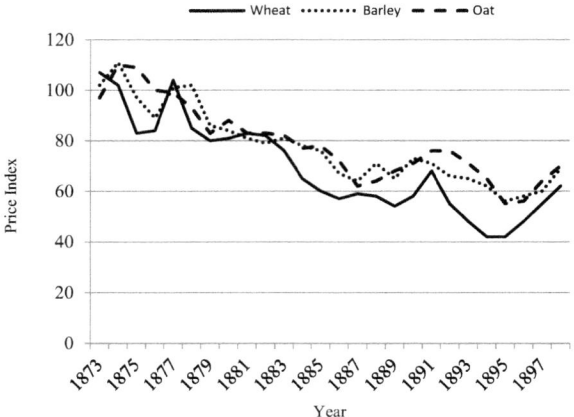

Chart 5.3 Farm prices, 1871–1898 (wool, 1871–5 = 100). *Source* Hunt and Pam (2002: 487)

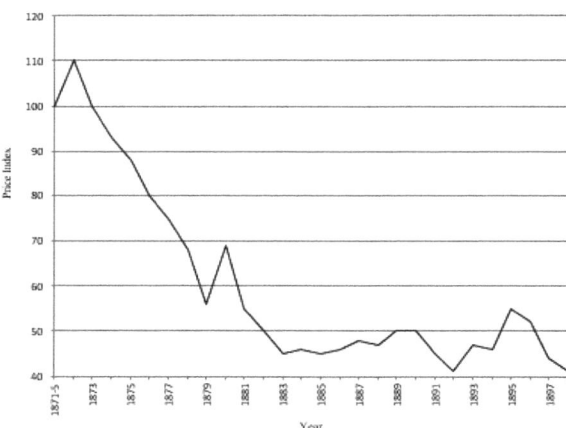

Chart 5.4 Wheat production in the UK, 1852–1891. *Source* NBER-Macrohistory Database Series (2020)

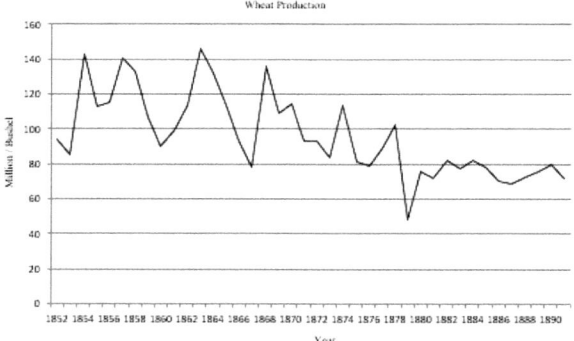

Chart 5.5 Wheat producing
areas in England,
1854–1891. *Source*
NBER-Macrohistory
Database Series (2020)

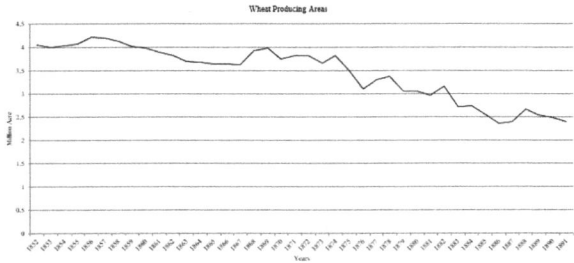

Chart 5.6 1873–1898 UK
agricultural products price
comparison (1871–5 = 100).
Source Derived from the
1873–1898 agricultural price
index (Hunt and Pam 2002:
480)

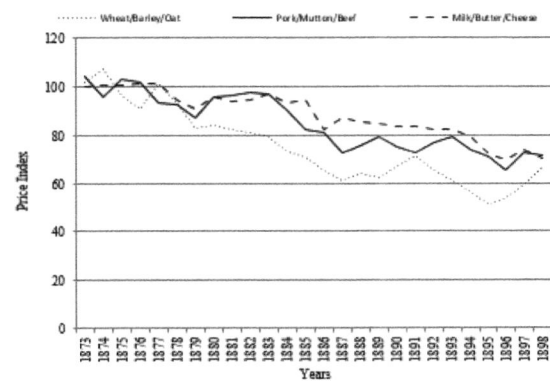

Although there was a similar decrease in oat and barley prices, most farmers
continued to grow these products for forage and basic hay needs.

Based on the aforementioned price index, it is understood that the products least
affected by price decreases are milk, butter and cheese, pork, beef and mutton
(Chart 5.5).

Finally, in Chart 5.6, the products in the aforementioned price index are divided
into three groups: wheat, barley, oats and milk, butter, cheese and pork, beef and
mutton, excluding wool, and they are compared on the basis of the average price
index of each group over the years. As can be seen by examining the chart in question,
it is clearly observed that the prices of agricultural products such as wheat, barley
and oats, which are considered as agricultural products, have declined dramatically
compared to foods of animal origin such as milk, butter, cheese and meat.

5.3   Conclusion

The long depression of 1873–1896 stands out as an important example in the history
of world crises that a financial problem in any country can easily affect other countries
due to the integrated international trade and financial system.

   The main feature of the crisis is that the unstable and long-term decline in product prices had a negative impact on profitability and investments, and this affected many countries and continents.

   As emphasized by Aldcroft and Musson, the most important consequence of the crisis that started in 1873 and lasted until 1896, including the periods of decline and recovery, the industry of the UK, which was the world industrial giant until 1873, slowed down and lost its leadership position to Germany and the USA, born as the new industrial powers. Although it spread to many countries, with different impacts, the country most affected by the crisis was the UK. At the same time, the dilemmas that the UK faced in the agricultural sector during this period caused the crisis to be felt more deeply in this country compared to other countries.

   On the other hand, economic activities and production volume continued to increase, albeit at a decreasing rate, despite the unstable long-term decline in prices. Although it continued until 1896, the fact that there were recovery periods for producers and investors during the crisis period and, from the point of consumers and wage earners, that real wages increased indirectly and enabled the redistribution of income, are considered as the other distinctive features of the period.

References

Akbaş ME (2017) 1800'lerin Küresel Krizleri, Büyük Depresyon ve 2008 Krizi. İGÜ Sos Bil Dergisi 4(1):77–127. https://dergipark.org.tr/en/download/article-file/293108

Aldcroft DH (1964) The entrepreneur and the British economy, 1870–1914. Econ Hist Rev 17(1):113–134. JSTOR. www.jstor.org/stable/2592694

Ashworth W (1965) Changes in the industrial structure: 1870–1914. Bull Econ Res 17:61–74. https://doi.org/10.1111/j.1467-8586.1965.tb00023.x

Balı S, Büyükşalvarcı A (2011) 1630'dan 2010'a Finansal Krizler Tarihi. Çatı Kitapları, İstanbul

Beales HL (1934) The Great Depression in industry and trade. Econ Hist Rev 5(1):65–75. JSTOR. https://www.jstor.org/stable/2589917

Britannica (2020) The German Empire, 1871–1914-the economy, 1870–1890. https://www.britan nica.com/place/Germany/The-economy-1870-90

Eğilmez M (2012) Kapitalizm ve Üç Büyük Krizi, Kendime Yazılar. Kişisel Blog. www.mahfiegil mez.com/2012/03/kapitalizm-ve-uc-buyuk-kriz.html

Fletcher TW (1961) The Great Depression of English agriculture, 1873–1896. Econ Hist Rev 13(3):417–432. JSTOR. https://www.jstor.org/stable/2599512

Gourevitch PA (1977) International Trade, Domestic Coalitions, and Liberty: Comparative Responses to the Crisis of 1873–1896. The Journal of Interdisciplinary History, vol. 8(2):281–313. Retrieved from: JSTOR. www.jstor.org/stable/202790

Hunt EH, Pam SJ (2002) Responding to agricultural depression, 1873–96: managerial success, entrepreneurial failure? Agric Hist Rev 50(2):225–252. JSTOR. www.jstor.org/stable/40275807

Kindleberger CP (1990) Historical economics: art or science? University of California Press, Berkeley

Marichal C (2009) World financial crises: lessons of the past. Finance Bien Commun, 34–35. https://doi.org/10.3917/fbc.034.0034. https://www.researchgate.net/publication/247908558

Mishkin F (1991) Asymmetric information and financial crises: a historical perspective. Financ Mark Financ Crises (National Bureau of Economic Research, Inc.) 69–108. https://www.nber.org/system/files/chapters/c11483/c11483.pdf

Musson AE (1959) The Great Depression in Britain, 1873–1896: a reappraisal. J Econ Hist 19(2):199–228. JSTOR. https://www.jstor.org/stable/2114975

NBER (2020) NBER macrohistory: NBER macrohistory database series from the United Kingdom. http://data.nber.org/databases/macrohistory/contents/uk.html

Pollard S (1985) Capital exports, 1870–1914: harmful or beneficial? Econ Hist Rev 38(4):489–514. https://doi.org/10.2307/2597185. JSTOR. https://www.jstor.org/stable/2597185

Rosenberg H (1943) Political and social consequences of the Great Depression of 1873–1896 in Central Europe. Econ Hist Rev 13(1/2):58–73. JSTOR. https://doi.org/10.2307/2590515. www.jstor.org/stable/2590515

Saul SB (1965) The export economy 1870–1914. Bull Econ Res 17:5–18. https://doi.org/10.1111/j.1467-8586.1965.tb00019.x

Turner M (1992) Output and prices in UK agriculture, 1867–1914, and the great agricultural depression reconsidered. Agric Hist Rev 40(1):38–51. JSTOR. www.jstor.org/stable/40274843

Wells O (1937) The depression of 1873–79. Agric Hist 11(3):237–251. JSTOR. www.jstor.org/stable/3739798

Wikipedia (2020a) Long depression. https://en.wikipedia.org/wiki/Long_Depression

Wikipedia (2020b) Great Depression of British agriculture. https://en.wikipedia.org/wiki/Great_Depression_of_British_Agriculture

Muhammet Kaya is a Ph.D. candidate at Izmir Katip Celebi University. He received his bachelor's degree in public administration from Izmir Dokuz Eylül University and his master's degree from Izmir Katip Celebi University. He also works as the Chief Inspector in The Ministry of Commerce of the Republic of Turkey. He served as the Vice President of Guidance and Inspection at the same ministry in 2011–2013. He has been conducting research, examination and investigation for approximately 21 years in the field of customs and foreign trade, including money laundering crimes. He was in England in 2010–2011 and 2015 for his language and professional development.

Chapter 6
Australian Banking Crisis of 1893

Muhammet Kaya

Abstract The Australian banking crisis of 1893 which is considered to be a long and intensely felt event in Australian history is an interesting example in terms of the history of the world economic crises in terms of showing the negative results that the free banking system may cause. The causes of the crisis are explained in the literature depending on internal and external causes. With this, the fact that Australian banks, which are almost not subject to any restrictions, turned to highly profitable land and mortgage banking apart from their normal banking activities, is shown as the main factor shaping the crisis.

Keywords Australian banking · Banking crises

6.1 Introduction

Although there are approaches based on internal and external factors in the literature to explain the reasons for the crisis, the Australian banking crisis of 1893 is an interesting example in terms of the history of the world economic crises in terms of showing the negative results that the free banking system may cause.

The financial crisis, which took effect from the end of the 1880s and reached its peak in 1893, is considered to be a long and intensely felt event in Australian history that led to a shrinkage of 17% in real GDP in 1891–1892 (Fitz-Gibbon and Gizycki 2001: 21).

The Australian banking crisis of 1893 will be examined by compiling the views on the factors that led to the crisis, and we will also include general information about Australia and the development of the banking system, which will be followed by the general picture before the crisis, and then focus on the emergence of the crisis and its causes.

M. Kaya (✉)
Department of Public Finance and Financial Management, Graduate School of Social Sciences, Izmir Katip Celebi University, İzmir, Turkey
e-mail: mkaya3576@gmail.com

© The Author(s), under exclusive license to Springer Nature Singapore Pte Ltd. 2022   79
B. Açıkgöz (ed.), *Black Swan: Economic Crises, Volume I*, Accounting, Finance, Sustainability, Governance & Fraud: Theory and Application,
https://doi.org/10.1007/978-981-19-5252-4_6

6.1.1 Australia

Australia, which had been home to Aboriginals, the original inhabitants of the continent for about 60,000 years before the immigration wave that began in 1788 when the UK established penal colonies in New South Wales (modern Sydney, Port Jackson), Tasmania (Van Diemen's Land) and Western Australia, is the 6th largest country in the world with a total area of $8,698,850 \text{ km}^2$, of which $8,617,930 \text{ km}^2$ on land and $80,920 \text{ km}^2$ in water. The first parts of the continent, all of which were discovered in the nineteenth century, were mapped by Dutch sailors in the seventeenth century, and by French and British sailors in the following century. The "forced immigration of convicts", initiated by the UK in 1788 in the form of penal transportation, was later replaced by an increasing number of free settlers, and thus a colony of purely free settlers was established in South Australia until the 1830s (Wikipedia 2020; Australian Government-DFAT 2020).

While the huge profit opportunities seen in livestock and mining in the process attracted substantial amounts of British capital to the country, economic expansion was shaped around large government spending on transport, communications, and urban infrastructures, mostly based on British funding. After New South Wales, four more British colonies were established under the name Western Australia in 1829, South Australia in 1836, Victoria in 1851 and Queensland in 1859, and these colonies had a responsible government, generally, in the 1850s (Self-Gutenberg 2020).

The gold discovered in South Wales and Victoria in the 1850s also initiated the process of bringing immigrants to Australia from all over the world with the slogan of "gold rush", thus Australia's total population, which was 430,000 in 1851, reached 1.7 million by 1871. With the flow of immigrants, especially the wealth provided by gold and wool brought along significant investments made in Melbourne and Sydney and developments that enabled the transformation of these settlements into modern cities. The small population of the country compared to the available land and resources played an important role in the rapid realization of economic growth with overseas exports, labour and capital inflows. By 1901, the (6) colonies in the region were united under the name of the Federal Commonwealth of Australia, and since then the country has been governed by a single constitution and constitutional monarchy. In Australia, which consists of six states and affiliated territories, the mining and agricultural sectors are the strengths of the country's economy and the country has a diversified economic structure in the production and service sectors (Self-Gutenberg 2020; Australian Government-DFAT 2020; Jackson 1977: 13).

Although the Australian Federal Community appeared as separate colonies and a combination of political governments similar to the US model before its establishment in 1901, in fact each colony displayed different stages of development. For example, although New South Wales, the oldest of these colonies, assumed management responsibility in 1856, Western Australia, which was small in terms of population and wealth but the largest in the region in terms of geographical area, did not have such an administrative structure until 1891. The development of all colonies was highly dependent on foreign credit, and the fiscal policies of each colony were also different. For example, New South Wales was governed under a free trade regime that allowed the development of secondary industries, while Victoria, having a crowded population, adopted protectionism economically. On the other hand, remote colonies such as Queensland, South Australia, Western Australia, and Tasmania also had secondary industries, but these colonies applied tariffs to generate income for other colonial neighbours and foreign countries (Q 1931: 477).

6.1.2 Australian Banking System

The Bank of New South Wales, the first bank of Australia, was established in 1817 by the colonial Governor Lachlan Macquarie in order to ensure stability in the colonial change system in the region and to support economic development as the subject to a corporate charter. In the 1820s, two more banks started operating in the New South West and Tasmanian colonies, which switched to the market economy. While the banks in the Australian colonies contributed to economic development, they also served as an important channel for the British and French capital inflow, increasing especially in the nineteenth century. It is claimed that these capital inflows contributed significantly to the economic development of Australia between 1860 and 1890 (Thomson Reuters 2020).

Although reference is often made to the free banking system, it is stated that Australian banks have never actually had a pure free banking experience but have relatively mild limitations compared to examples elsewhere. Australian banks, which were free from significant government intervention until the 1890s, were not subject to any restrictions on entry to the system, with a few legal barriers, nor were they subject to any reliable restrictions or legally established price controls on bank assets, debts, or capital. On the other hand, there was no deposit guarantee provided by the central bank or the state in the banking system. Nevertheless, all these features make the Australian banking of the period a good example of the free banking system (Hickson and Turner 2002: 147; Dowd 1993: 108).

While it will be detailed later, according to Hickson and Turner, the instability attributed to Australian banking is also explained by the lack of restrictions on more lending and over-risky investment. In this context, regulations faced by Australian banks in the name of restriction consist of the double liability imposed on bank owners and the limitation of the printing of banknotes to their paid-in capital. As Hickson and Turner cite from Woodward, although the double liability for bank owners required the restriction of share transfer, there was no such requirement in Australia and bank shares could be freely transferred (Hickson and Turner 2004: 909).

On the other hand, before 1893, Australian banks stood out with their land and mortgage banking identities rather than their normal banking activities. Investing in real estate mortgages and risky securities is the distinguishing feature of Australian banks in this period. According to Ellis, although the specified activities require serious capital, they actually attract attention as highly profitable investment areas (Ellis 1893: 494).

On the other hand, it is claimed that the basis of the Australian free banking system is the Colonial Bank Regulations that were put into practice in 1840 and revised in 1846. Prior to these regulations, Australian banks, which had unlimited liabilities, were limited to six partners. This restriction prevented banks from investing in risky assets. Until 1846, bank supervision responsibility belonged to the relevant colonial government, yet with the introduction of regulations on that date, all Australian banks except Western Australia were granted autonomy in banking. However, it should be noted that since 1862, the colonial banking system was no longer controlled by the British Treasury. Although, with the Colonial Bank Regulations, basic restrictions were imposed such as banknote issuance being limited to bank paid-in capital, unlimited share liability for bond issuance, doubling the paid-in capital for all public debts, and not allowing progress on real estate, especially after 1862, it was argued that the colonies, while generally complying with these regulations, did not actually significantly restrict or change bank behavior. For example, the restrictions imposed on real estate were somewhat overcome by legal methods, especially in Victoria, the restrictions on this issue were lifted in 1888 with the belief that they were ineffective (Hickson and Turner 2002: 152–154).

The Australian banking system was essentially shaped by the British model and as noted, banks in general faced few restrictions on protecting their branch and agency networks. In Australia, 58 commercial banks were opened between 1817 and 1914, and the maximum number of banks open at any given time was 31 in 1890. Although the initial increase in the number of offices was slow due to the sparse settlement of the colonies, the number of branches increased rapidly from the 1850s, especially in Victoria, where Melbourne emerged as the colonies' financial center. Out of 178 branches, only 96 were in Victoria in 1859. It is claimed that the number of branches and assets of commercial banks increased more than seven times between 1866 and 1890 (Seltzer 2018: 341–342).

Although this was the case, Dowd stated that branching allows banks to save on operating costs such as holding less reserves on one hand, and on the other hand to provide some special services such as foreign currency equivalents at a lower cost, as well as providing protection against adverse conditions in their regions by diversifying risks (Dowd 1993: 111).

6.2 Crisis and Pre-crisis General Outlook

With the effect of the wealth coming from gold and wool especially, which brought immigrants from all over the world to Australia since 1851, the high economic growth rates that emerged from the 1860s made the colonies attractive for British investors, as well. In this framework, as cited by Hickson and Turner, the moderate capital inflow entering the country until 1880 was evaluated as a flood in the period between

1881 and 1885 and as a deluge in the period between 1885 and 1890 (Hickson and Turner 2002: 149).

By 1890, Australia's economic expansion gave way to instability. The balance of payments, on the other hand, is shown as the source of serious deflationary pressures in the early 1890s. Export revenues decreased by 12–13% between 1891 and 1894, especially with the effect of the decrease in wool prices. Capital inflow, which became almost necessary to maintain continuity in economic development, declined more than exports, thus capital inflow entering the country this way in the first half of the 1890s was only around a quarter of the capital entering the country until the late 1880s (Jackson 1977: 23).

According to Hickson and Turner, remarkable speculative movements from the 1880s until 1893, when the banking crisis broke out, led to rapid and significant increases in the stocks of companies operating in the fields of real estate prices, land, land financing and mining. For example, compared to the previous year, it is observed that the volume of shares traded in the Melbourne Stock Exchange increased three times in 1888 data. As the underlying reason for this speculation is considered to be the rate of increase in the amount of capital coming from overseas countries such as the UK and Scotland during the period 1886 and 1890, especially to commercial banks, pastoral companies, and land and finance companies. Such that the amount of foreign capital, which constituted 12.8% of the total bank deposits in 1880, increased to 27.1% in 1891 (Hickson and Turner 2002: 150).

6.3   Australian Banking Crisis of 1893 and Its Background

The Australian financial system turning to the land and mortgage market towards the 1880s paved the way for increasingly obtained funds domestically and especially from the UK by Australian financial intermediaries, the most important of which were the commercial banks, to be transformed into the building and pastoral industry by real estate banks, building cooperatives and pastoral finance companies (Merrett 2013: 409–410).

However, the fact that the money supply from overseas countries exceeded the existing demand in the colonies started a cycle that created a land and company explosion that caused a fictitious spike in the value of almost all properties in the region (Hickson and Turner 2002: 148).

According to Merret, the speculation that started in the 1880s attracted considerable attention in urban real estates, especially in Melbourne, the capital of Victoria, and contains evidence of excessive investment in the pastoral industry and public services during this period. As the capital inflows from overseas countries increased the balance sheets of both intermediaries and their customers, the ratio of loans to gross domestic product increased considerably (Merrett 2013: 409–410).

According to Hickson and Turner, until before the crisis, all commercial banks in Australia have extensively provided loans to land financing companies, mortgage companies, companies, and individuals engaged in speculative transactions in property and stock exchanges, due to the capital entering the country especially from the UK. However, the widespread bankruptcy of companies and deposit outflows due to the sudden cut-off of the deposits entering the country in 1888 created a significant burden and pressure on commercial banks. Land mortgage companies, known as "zombies" until 1891 could not survive with the gradual decrease in the entry of British deposits; however, many real estate companies survived with the loans they received from Australian commercial banks, thanks to the limited deposits from the UK. Yet, due to the fact that commercial banks could not lend to land mortgage companies due to the increase in the cost of deposits obtained from the UK, from 1891 to March 1892, only 41 land financing companies in Melbourne and Sydney went bankrupt (Hickson and Turner 2002: 148).

Thus, asset prices, which melted due to the contraction in commodity prices, increased the pressure on borrowers, which started to undermine the stability of lending financial institutions. The failures of real estate banks and building cooperatives between 1891 and 1892 fueled the fears of commercial bank depositors. In particular, it is stated that the suspension and liquidation of the Australian Commercial Bank and the Australian Federal Bank, closely related to the building cooperatives on 5 March 1892 and 28 January 1893 increased concern over the security of 22 other banks, but the bank shareholders emptied the stocks long before depositors began seeking safe havens. It is reported that, in Melbourne, the epicenter of the speculative building boom, the Australian Commercial Bank, the largest bank in the Victoria colony, was closed on 5 April 1893, as a result of the developments, and within six weeks, 13 out of Australia's 22 commercial banks were suspended, although the situation was not so bright for others (Hickson and Turner 2002: 149; Merrett 2013: 410).

According to Jackson, as a result of the crisis of 1893, Australia's gross domestic product declined by up to 20% between 1891 and 1895, while per capita product fell to less than three-quarters of the peak levels of the 1880s in the mid-1890s. Again, the contraction in economic activities of this scale arising from this crisis, which caused the collapse of many financial institutions and turmoil between banks and caused significant commercial and financial difficulties, resulted in high unemployment rates with significant declines in nominal and real wages. According to him, the depression in question in the 1890s was much more severe and lasted longer than the crises and depressions such as the 1840 depression Australia had previously experienced (Jackson 1977: 23).

6.3.1   Causes of the Crisis

As mentioned, the reasons for the reversal of things and the depression experienced since 1888 are detailed in the literature by focusing on internal and external factors.

While the collapse of Barings in London in 1890 and the sharp decline in wool prices are shown as external factors, the weaknesses in financial and commercial matters and the fact that the banking system and its functioning were not subject to any legal obstacles or restrictions, other than some restrictions, i.e., the free banking system are mentioned as internal factors.

Among the external factors, the Baring crisis is associated with the Franco-Prussian war and the German economy. In this context, Germany, which accelerated its economy thanks to the huge war reparations it received from France after the Franco-Prussian war, suddenly stopped the loan it provided to Argentina for the large water treatment project worth £3.5 million, which resulted in Argentina and the British Baring Brother Bank, which provided the support, hit by a financial crisis, and this development included the related countries and companies in the crisis cycle. Despite the suspension of Germany's loan to Argentina, the British Barings Bank, which continued its financial support to this country, went bankrupt because it did not take into account the warnings of the British Central Bank on this issue. Since Barings' bankruptcy caused concerns in capital outflows from the UK to overseas countries, it caused a decrease in capital outflows to these countries or the conditions for financial support were tightened. These restrictions and tight measures shortly led to a crisis in countries whose financial system was highly indexed to the British capital, such as Australia (Desai 2004: 11–12).

Wool export had an important place in the export revenues of Australia from the very beginning. It is observed that 82% of Australian exports were directed to the UK in the years 1848–1850 and 67% of total exports consisted of only wool exports, and by the 1890s this rate remained its proportional weight which was 66% (Jackson 1977: 7–21).

The long depression of 1873–1896, which coincided with the Australian crisis of 1893, marks the period in which serious falls in product prices all over the world. This period, especially when wheat and wool prices crashed, had negative consequences for Australia in terms of the income to be obtained from wool exports, which had a significant weight in total exports, and therefore the balance of payments.

Butlin and Bohem, Merret, Ellis and Dowd have various opinions on the structural weaknesses specific to the banking system. In this framework, according to the citations by Hickson and Turner; Butlin and Boehm pointed out that a significant portion of bank assets was locked into real estate mortgages, many banks had low liquidity standards, and British deposits were seen as different from other colonial deposits, and the increased competition for new business in the period between 1880 and 1890 fueled branch banking, while Merret pointed out that the increasing number of branches due to competition worsened the prudent standards of banks, similarly, weak internal controls, maturity mismatches, declining asset quality, overly concentrated risks, weak liquidity standards and insufficient capital are also other practices that accelerate the deterioration of these standards. On the other hand, Ellis argued that the government intervention shaped by the crisis essentially partially led to it or at least exacerbated it, Dowd argued that the reconstructions authorized by the colonial governments encouraged a legal suspension case that allowed banks to rebuild under favorable conditions and that the Victorian Treasurer's attempts to force associated banks to help weak banks seriously undermined public trust; again, at the beginning of May 1893 the bank holiday imposed by the Victorian government also weakened public confidence. However, contrary to Dowd, Hickson and Turner argued that not the management strategies in question but the erroneous methods applied contributed to the crisis as the main cause of the crisis (Hickson and Turner 2002: 150–151).

Hickson and Turner argue that the crisis occurred because the banks' opportunistic capacities were not efficiently curtailed by the legislature, as a result of which the real shock occurred when the crisis impacted the banking system, as the underlying weaknesses emerged. Accordingly, Australian banks operated in a regulatory environment that allowed their management to over-expand their institutions if they wished, by increasing their deposits, reducing levels of liquid reserves held against deposits, and investing large proportions of their loan portfolios in exceptionally risky assets. They based their claims on the differences between the surviving banks and the banks that collapsed, based on individual bank balance sheet data (Hickson and Turner 2002: 151–152).

As discussed in the previous chapters, it was shown as a distinctive feature of the period that before the crisis, Australian banks turned to land and mortgage banking, which required a significant amount of capital other than normal banking activities but had a very high-profit yield (Ellis 1893: 494).

It was suggested that the effect of almost unrestricted competition in the fields of activity of Australian banks was great on banks' turning to mortgage and land banking other than their normal banking activities. The unlimited competition in question paved the way for the rapid expansion of the banks, which led to the collapse of the land boom in the 1880s and the banks were dragged into a crisis (Dowd 1993: 108).

On the other hand, as Gibbon and Gizycki reported from Merrett, although the land boom that started in the 1880s was financed by credit expansion, many building cooperatives and real estate financing companies are known as "Àland Banksî" also emerged in these years. Increasing competition from these new types of companies played an important role in weakening the prudent standards of banks (Fitz-Gibbon and Gizycki 2001: 21).

From 1850 to 1880 Australian banking expanded significantly. According to Dowd, during this period, especially savings banks were supported by colonial governments as they were seen as a means of providing cheap loans. Evidence of this expansion is the improvement in banknote printing, deposits and loans between 1850 and 1860. Banknote printing increased from £447,000 in the first quarter of 1851 to £3,192,000 in ten years, and deposits from £2,932,000 to £14,538,000. Loans increased at a similar rate in the same period. Again, as Dowd cited from Pope, the environment of the 1870s and 1880s was also very suitable for the expansion of branch banking. Australian banks, which promised higher interest rates compared to the UK, were very attractive to British investors and were a relatively cheap source of funding for banks. As a result of this favorable environment, the share of British deposits, which were 10% in Australian deposits in the mid-1870s, increased to 40% during the depression period (Dowd 1993: 113–114).

The extent of the credit expansion toward the crisis period can be clearly seen from the data on the ratio of bank loans to GDP in the Australian colonies in 1880 and

Table 6.1 Bank advances as proportion of nominal GDP in 1880 and 1892 by Colony and Australia

Years	New South Wales	Victoria	Queensland	South Australia	Western Australia	Tasmania	Australia
1880	34.2	39.4	35.6	29.2	28.6	26.3	34.0
1892	59.5	89.8	91.6	52.1	64.7	40.8	73.7

Source Merrett (2013: 418)

1892 given in Table 6.1 compiled by Merrett from various sources. It is understood that the said increase is higher especially in Victoria and Queensland.

According to Gairdner, the inevitable collapse of 1893 should not be surprising. The difficulties faced by banks were aggravated by the amount of loans transferred to small communities through different channels. The large sums borrowed by colonial governments, municipalities, mortgage companies and trading companies in the last ten or fifteen years were not able to be absorbed and used beneficially in addition to the increasing bank deposits. Hence, prices and wages were overly inflated, and capital was spent for many purposes that were not urgent or needed (Gairdner 1894: 119).

As shown in Table 6.2, the increase in Australian bank deposits as a percentage of total assets in the period of 1862–1892 stands out. As can be seen from the aforementioned data displayed in the table, the Australian banking system is largely based on deposits. Therefore, it is suggested that the bond issue restriction will have little effect on banks' risk-taking (Hickson and Turner 2002: 153) (Chart 6.1).

In the aforementioned chart, it is revealed that the specified rate has decreased after the end of the control, especially since 1862. Based on the study conducted by Hickson and Turner, it is stated that the average equity/deposit ratio for the surviving banks is significantly higher compared to the failed or suspended banks (Hickson and Turner 2002: 158).

Table 6.2 The note and deposit issue of Australian banking system, 1862–92

	Deposit/Assets (%)	Notes/Total assets (%)
1862	47.40	8.63
1872	55.90	5.16
1882	65.59	4.45
1892	71.29	2.29

Source Hickson and Turner (2002: 153)

Chart 6.1 Equity/Deposit ratio for Australian banks, 1862–92. *Source* Hickson and Turner (2002: 158)

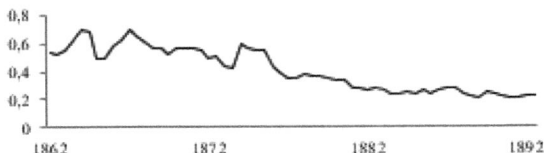

Charts on the number of banks and branches in Australia between the years 1817–1914 are included in Charts 6.2 and 6.3.

As it can be understood from Charts 6.3 and 6.4, it is obvious that the number of both banks and branches gradually increased especially since 1850s. Banking and branching, which peaked until 1893, had a sharp decline since then.

The average liquid assets/total assets ratio for Australian banks is as shown in Chart 6.4. Based on this chart, Hickson and Turner stated that the cost to cover sharp increases in deposit outflows during the crisis period increased significantly, and that suspended or failed banks had significantly lower liquid reserve levels than survivors (Hickson and Turner 2002: 159).

Chart 6.2 Number of trade banks in Australia, 1817–1914. *Source* Seltzer (2018: 342)

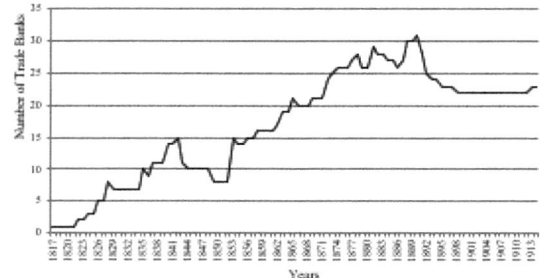

Chart 6.3 Number of trade banks branches in Australia, 1817–1914. *Source* Seltzer (2018: 342)

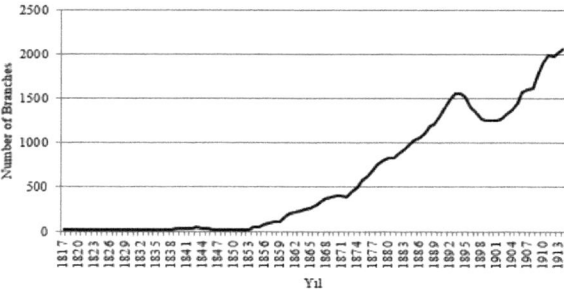

Chart 6.4 Average liquid assets/total assets ratio for Australian banks, 1862–92. *Source* Hickson and Turner (2002: 159)

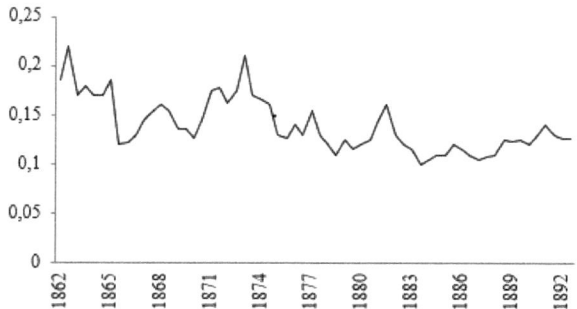

Table 6.3 Source of Australian bank deposits, 1870–92

	Deposits from Australia (£m)	Deposits from Australia/total assets (%)	Deposits from overseas (£m)	Deposits from overseas/total assets (%)	Deposits from overseas as % of total deposits
1870	19.1	45.9	2.6	6.3	12.0
1875	32.3	52.3	3.6	5.8	10.0
1880	44.2	58.6	6.5	8.6	12.8
1885	73.4	57.5	16.8	13.2	18.6
1888	88.5	54.0	24.0	14.6	22.8
1889	92.2	53.2	29.8	17.2	24.4
1890	97.6	53.6	33.4	18.4	25.5
1891	97.7	52.8	36.3	19.6	27.1
1892	98.6	53.4	33.6	18.2	25.4

Source Hickson and Turner (2002: 158)

Table 6.3 contains data regarding the growth of British deposits in Australian banks. Hickson and Turner noted that the average British deposits held by failed or suspended banks were significantly higher than those of surviving banks. According to them, some commentators think that a large amount of UK deposits in the Australian banking system is one of the major weaknesses (Hickson and Turner 2002: 158).

The study by Hickson and Turner also provides evidence that indicates banks' exposure to increased risk, as well as the recklessness of Australian bank management in their lending activities. According to Hickson and Turner, it is a common view that banks lend too much to land, property, and shares, and Peel estimated that, in 1890–92, 20% of bank advances included land and property loans and 67% were considerations for pastoral securities. The rapid decline in the value of such securities at the end of the 1880s would lead to a significant increase in the amount of loan defaults (Hickson and Turner 2002: 158).

A similar approach to the stated point of view is shared by Jackson, Fitz-Gibbon and Gizycki. Accordingly, the beginning of the collapse dates back to the end of the 1880s. The abrupt cessation of the land boom in metropolitan areas left many land and construction companies with short-term liabilities and unreasonable assets. Assuming that the recession was temporary, the solution which is increasing the short-term debt of these companies with new liabilities from the banking system would only be possible with the easy credit conditions supported by the ongoing capital inflow and the recovery of the land market. But as it became clear that the fall in property prices was not just a temporary fluctuation, the financial collapse spread to land banks. In 1891 and 1892, the increase in the loss of trust in these companies caused the withdrawal of bank deposits, while at the same time, the financial system was doomed to failure in a short time (Jackson 1977: 146; Fitz-Gibbon and Gizycki 2001: 22).

6.3.2   Post-crisis Period

It was stated by Merrett that the post-crisis period witnessed restructuring plans, bargains between bank creditors and owners, banking activities continued, the private costs of the parties spread to the real economy, and the decrease in the wealth of depositors and shareholders also reduced expenditures (Merrett 2013: 428).

Hickson and Turner stated that after the crisis of 1893, no action could be taken, although proposals were made for the establishment of state banks and uniform banking laws in all colonies. After the establishment of the Australian Federal Community in 1901, although a series of orders were given on this issue, the excessive risky behaviors of the banks were mainly tried to be overcome by the threat of loan removal (Hickson and Turner 2002: 151–152).

According to Jackson, the crisis of 1893 emerges as a result rather than being a serious economic crisis. The banks that survived the restructuring period followed more cautious lending policies and adopted higher reserve ratios than before the crisis. On the other hand, in this period, both deposit and loan interest rates were considerably lower than the previous period standards. For example, while the interest rates applied to twelve-month fixed deposits were around 2.5–3% between 1896 and 1900, this rate was 5% on average during the land boom in the 1880s. On the other hand, although it was not deemed profitable to seek new deposit opportunities in the UK during this period, gradual repayment of old deposits significantly decreased the amount of British funds in the banking system (Jackson 1977: 148).

On the other hand, after the crisis of 1893, deposits lost their market share to commercial and savings banks and life insurance offices, and they barely reached their deposit levels of 1893 until 1903. However, the savings bank deposits almost doubled during this period and grew by 61% until 1913 (Merrett 2013: 424).

6.4   Conclusion

The Australian banking crisis of 1893 sets a unique example in the history of the world economic crises in terms of the adverse effects of the free banking system, where there is an excessive risk appetite in the free banking system and there is no legal obstacle other than exceptional restrictions.

The main factors shaping the development of the crisis are the facts that the land and building boom of the 1880s combined with the excessive risk appetite of banks that are not subject to restraint, and that banks turn to land and mortgage banking, which requires a high amount of capital but is highly profitable, other than their normal banking activities.

Although it is seen as a unique example, the financial crisis of 1893 also emerges as another example that is necessary to be learned from, as is the case for other financial crises, as it reveals that speculative transactions and activities of unrestricted or uncontrolled economic units will eventually bring about economic deterioration.

References

Australian Government, Department of Foreign Affairs and Trade-DFAT (2020) History. https://www.dfat.gov.au/about-australia/land-its-people/Pages/history

Desai M (2004) Financial crises and global governance, M. Desai & Y. Said in global governance and financial crises. Routledge Publishing, London and New York, pp 6–18

Dowd K (1993) Laissez-faire banking. Routledge Publishing, Routledge, London and New York

Ellis A (1893) The Australian banking crisis. Econ J 3(10):293–297. https://doi.org/10.2307/2955673. https://www.jstor.org/stable/2955673

Fitz-Gibbon B, Gizycki M (2001) A history of last-resort lending and other support for troubled financial institutions in Australia. Reserve Bank of Australia, RBA Research Discussion Papers

Gairdner C (1894) The lessons of the Australian banking collapse. Econ J 4(13):114–119. https://doi.org/10.2307/2955880. JSTOR. https://www.jstor.org/stable/2955880

Hickson C, Turner J (2002) Free banking gone awry: the Australian banking crisis of 1893. Financ Hist Rev 9(2):147–167. https://doi.org/10.1017/S0968565002000124

Hickson C, Turner J (2004) Free banking and the stability of early joint-stock banking. Camb J Econ 28(6):903–919. JSTOR. www.jstor.org/stable/23602149

Jackson RV (1977) Australian economic development in the nineteenth century. National University Press, Canberra

Merrett DT (2013) The Australian bank crashes of the 1890s revisited. Bus Hist Rev 87(3):407–429. https://doi.org/10.1017/S0007680513000706. https://www.jstor.org/stable/43299162

Q (1931) The Australian crisis. Foreign Aff 9(3):477–486. JSTOR. www.jstor.org/stable/20030372

Self-Gutenberg (2020) Economic history of Australia. http://self.gutenberg.org/articles/eng/Economic_history_of_Australia. Accessed 02 June 2020

Seltzer A (2018) The functions of Australian banks' branch networks: the diversification of risks and spatial allocation of capital. Aust Econ Hist Rev 58(3):338–361

Thomson Reuters (2020) Banking (Part 1): a very short history—updated commentary in TLA. https://support.thomsonreuters.com.au/product/westlaw-au/updates-alerts/banking-part-1-very-short-history-updated-commentary-tla. Accessed 14 April 2020

Wikipedia (2020) Australia. https://tr.wikipedia.org/wiki/Avustralya

Muhammet Kaya is a Ph.D. candidate at Izmir Katip Celebi University. He received his bachelor's degree in public administration from Izmir Dokuz Eylül University and his master's degree from Izmir Katip Celebi University. He also works as the Chief Inspector in The Ministry of Commerce of the Republic of Turkey. He served as the Vice President of Guidance and Inspection at the same ministry in 2011–2013. He has been conducting research, examination and investigation for approximately 21 years in the field of customs and foreign trade, including money laundering crimes. He was in England in 2010–2011 and 2015 for his language and professional development.

Index

Printed by Printforce, the Netherlands